Hands-On Activities **With Scripture Values**

LEVEL D

STUDENT WORKTEXT

ISBN #1-58938-143-2

Published by The Concerned Group, Inc.
700 East Granite • PO Box 1000 • Siloam Springs, AR 72761

Authors	**Dave & Rozann Seela**
Publisher	**Russ L. Potter, II**
Senior Editor	**Bill Morelan**
Project Coordinator	**Rocki Vanatta**
Creative Director	**Daniel Potter**
Proofreader	**Elizabeth Granderson**
Step Illustrations	**Steven Butler**
Character Illustrations	**Josh Ray**
Colorists	**Josh & Aimee Ray**

Printed on recycled paper in the United States

For more information about A Reason For® curricula,
write to the address above, call, or visit our website.

www.areasonfor.com
800.447.4332

Dear Parent,

Welcome to a new school year! This letter is to introduce you to **A Reason For©** Science.

A Reason For© Science teaches basic Life, Earth, and Physical Science through fun, hands-on activities. Each lesson is tied directly to the **National Science Education Content Standards** and uses an inquiry-based approach designed to enhance learning.

Today's increasingly complex world requires a clear understanding of science and technology. Our future prosperity depends on helping children rediscover the challenges, excitement, and joy of science — especially in the context of Scripture values. Thus, one of the primary goals of **A Reason For©** Science is to make science not only meaningful, but also FUN!

Fun, Flexible Format

Instead of a hardback textbook filled with "facts" to memorize, your child will be working in an interactive worktext designed to develop critical-thinking skills. Students start each week with a hands-on activity demonstrating a key science concept. This is followed by group discussion, journaling, and a series of thought-provoking questions. Lessons conclude with a summary of key concepts and a related "object lesson" from Scripture.

Safety Issues

The hands-on nature of **A Reason For©** Science means your child will be working with age-appropriate materials. (For instance, the "acids" we use are actually dilute forms comparable to typical household chemicals.) Like a field trip or gym class, these science activities usually require simple safety precautions.

But for instructional reasons, all materials in **A Reason For©** Science are treated as hazardous! This encourages students to develop good safety habits for use in later years. (If you have further questions about safety, your child's teacher has an in-depth safety manual outlining precautions for every lesson.)

Scripture Values

Best of all, **A Reason For©** Science features Scripture values! Every lesson concludes with a Scripture object lesson related to the week's topic. These "Food for Thought" sections encourage students to relate everyday experiences to Scriptural themes, providing a positive way to integrate faith and learning.

Here's to an exciting year exploring God's world!

Dave & Rozann Seela
Authors, **A Reason For©** Science

A Reason For© Science makes science FUN! Your school year will be filled with hands-on activities, colorful discovery sheets, and lots of discussion and exploration. You'll discover many exciting new things as you explore God's world!

Although "almost everything relates to everything else" in some way or another, scientists usually divide science into three broad areas for study: life, earth, and physical science. The sections in your worktext are based on these categories.

Colorful icons are used to help you identify each section. An **ant** represents **Life Science** lessons. A **globe** stands for **Earth Science** lessons. An **atom** introduces **Physical Science (Energy/Matter)** lessons. And a **hammer** represents the **Physical Science (Forces)** lessons.

Life Science

Life Science is the study of **living things.** In the Life Science section of your **A Reason For©** Science worktext, you'll explore different kinds of living things. You'll learn about their characteristics (how they're alike or different). You'll discover how scientists classify (label and sort) living things. You'll even learn more about your own body and how it works!

Earth Science

Earth Science is the study of **earth** and **sky**. In the Earth Science section of your **A Reason For©** Science worktext, you'll explore the structure of our planet (rocks, crystals, volcanos), the atmosphere (air, clouds), and related systems (water cycles, air pressure, weather). Grades 7 and 8 reach out even further with a look at the solar system and stars.

Physical Science

Physical Science is the study of energy, matter, and related forces. Since the physical part of science has a big effect on your daily life, it's divided into two major sections:

Energy and Matter

In this section of your **A Reason For**© Science worktext, you'll learn about the different states and unique properties of matter. You'll discover new things about light and sound. You'll explore physical and chemical reactions. Some grades will explore related concepts like circuits, currents, and convection.

Forces

In this section of your **A Reason For**© Science worktext, you'll discover how "push and pull" form the basis for all physical movement. You'll explore simple machines (levers, pulleys). You'll work with Newton's laws of motion. You'll even learn to understand concepts like torque, inertia, and buoyancy.

Safety First!

Before you begin, be sure to read about "Peat" the safety worm. Peat's job is to warn you whenever there's a potential hazard around. (Whenever you see Peat and his warning sign, STOP and wait for further instructions from your teacher!)

Exploring God's world of science often requires using equipment or materials that can injure you if they're not handled correctly. Also, many accidents occur when people hurry, are careless, or ignore safety rules.

It's your responsibility to know and observe the rules and to use care and caution as you work. Just like when you're on the playground, horseplay or ignoring safety rules can be dangerous. Don't let an accident happen to you!

Meet "Peat" the Safety Worm!
Peat's job is to warn you whenever there's a potential hazard around. Whenever you see Peat and his warning sign, **STOP** and wait for further instructions from your teacher!

Peat's sign helps you know what kind of hazard is present. Before beginning each activity, your teacher will discuss this hazard in detail and review the safety rules that apply.

means this activity requires **PROTECTIVE GEAR.**

Usually **gloves** or **goggles** (or both) are required. Goggles protect your eyes from things like flying debris or splashing liquids. Gloves protect your hands from things like heat, broken glass, or corrosive chemicals.

means there is a BURN HAZARD. There are three common burn hazards.

"Open Flame" indicates the presence of fire (often matches or a candle). "Thermal Burn" means objects may be too hot to touch. "Corrosion" indicates a chemical substance is present.

means there is a POISON HAZARD.

There are three common poison hazards. "Skin Contact" indicates a substance that should not touch skin. "Vapor" indicates fumes that should not be inhaled. "Hygiene" indicates the presence of materials that may contain germs.

indicates OTHER HAZARDS.

There are three additional hazards that require caution. **"Breakage"** indicates the presence of fragile substances (like glass). **"Slipping"** indicates liquids that might spill on the floor. **"Sharp Objects"** indicates the presence of tools with sharp edges or points.

Play It Safe!

Exploring God's world with A Reason For© Science can be great fun, but remember — play it safe! Observe all the safety rules, handle equipment and materials carefully, and always be cautious and alert.

And don't forget Peat the safety worm! Whenever you see Peat and his warning sign, **STOP** and wait for further instructions from your teacher.

Life Science

Life Science is the study of **living things.** In this section, you'll explore different kinds of living things. You'll learn about their characteristics (how they're alike or different). You'll discover how scientists classify (label and sort) living things. You'll even learn more about your own body and how it works!

SEARCHING SPROUTS

FOCUS Germination

OBJECTIVE To explore the process of growth in plants

OVERVIEW We know that animals behave in different ways depending on their surroundings. But do plants behave in different ways, too? In this activity, we'll explore some things that might have an impact on how plants behave.

WHAT TO DO

STEP 1

Place a petri dish on a paper towel. **Mark** around the bottom of the dish, then **cut** the towel just inside the lines to make a circle. **Make** three circles and **place** them in the bottom of three dishes. **Tape** to secure.

STEP 2

Tape six seeds to each towel. (Make sure they are all facing the same way.) Now **add** enough water to make the towel soggy. **Put** the lid on each dish and **tape** it shut. **Place** them in a warm, sunny spot as your teacher directs.

STEP 3

Carefully **observe** the dishes of seeds. (One is lying flat; one is on edge, seeds up; one is on edge, seeds upside down.) **Predict** which direction the seeds will grow. Be sure to **record** your predictions in your journal.

STEP 4

Examine the dishes each day. (Don't change their position in any way!) Seeds should sprout in a day or two. **Record** the direction leaves and roots grow. At the end of the week, **share** and **compare** observations with your research team.

WHAT HAPPENED?

Your plants displayed some very specific behaviors as they began to grow. This kind of plant **behavior** is called a **tropism**. Notice that no matter which way a seed was facing, the leaves always tried to point toward the **light**. Light is their **energy** source — they need it to make food. A seed only has a limited food supply for the **embryo** (baby plant) to use. Without sunlight, the young plant will die because this stored food doesn't last very long.

The roots followed gravity in the opposite direction from the leaves. Roots have two main functions: to **anchor** (hold down) the plant, and to **absorb** water and **nutrients**. As the top of the plant grows up, the roots grow down. This keeps the plant from tipping over, or from being washed or blown away. Also, if an animal comes along and eats the plant's top, the roots often can start another new plant!

WHAT WE LEARNED

1 In Step 1, you placed paper towel circles in the petri dish. What purpose did these serve? Why were they important?

_____

_____

_____

_____

_____

_____

_____

2 In Step 3, what did you predict? How did your prediction compare to what actually happened?

_____

_____

_____

_____

_____

_____

_____

3 Why do you think one dish had to lie flat? Why was it important to have a "control" set for comparison?

_____

_____

_____

_____

_____

_____

4 Describe what happened in the dishes during Step 4.

_____

_____

_____

_____

_____

_____

_____

5 Why was it important for the plants to behave as they did? What might happen if they didn't behave this way?

_____

_____

_____

_____

_____

_____

! CONCLUSION

Plants respond to their environment with specific behaviors. God created these behaviors in animals and plants to help them survive.

FOOD FOR THOUGHT

2 Thessalonians 3:4-5 No matter which direction the seeds were planted, up was up and down was down! Plants respond to what is around them, and this behavior is vital to their survival.

Our parents and teachers give us important directions, too. They want us to be safe, to get a good education, and most of all to follow Jesus. Even more important are the directions that come from God. This Scripture reminds us not only to hear God's word, but also to put it into practice! Let's learn from the plants and always face in the right direction.

JOURNAL My Science Notes

_____

_____

_____

_____

_____

_____

_____

_____

_____

_____

_____

_____

_____

_____

_____

_____

_____

_____

NAME _____

FEARSOME FANGS

FOCUS Classification

OBJECTIVE To explore how characteristics are used for identification

OVERVIEW Some snakes are poisonous, and some are not. Obviously, it's good to know the difference! Since bringing live poisonous snakes to class isn't a good idea, we'll rely on drawings and descriptions for this activity.

WHAT TO DO

STEP 1

Remove the "Fearsome Fangs" page from the back of your worktext (page 163). **Note** that some of these snakes are poisonous and some are not. **Discuss** similarities and differences in how these snakes look with your research team.

STEP 2

Place a white sock on one hand to make a snake puppet. Use colored markers to make it look like one of the non-poisonous snakes. **Examine** your snake puppet. In your journal, **record** observations about this snake.

STEP 3

Replace the first sock with the second. **Color** it to look like a poisonous snake. **Slip** two plastic pipettes filled with water into the sock. **Poke** the tips through the sock into the top of the mouth. **Examine** your poisonous puppet. **Record** observations about this snake.

STEP 4

Using your poisonous puppet, **bite** your other hand. (Don't bite hard!) As you bite, **squeeze** the bulbs. **Observe** how the fangs work. This is how poisonous snakes inject their venom into their prey! Now **share** and **compare** observations with your research team.

WHAT HAPPENED?

Some people think all snakes are bad. But can you imagine what might happen if there were no snakes to keep the rodent population down? Mice and rats could be everywhere! Remember, God created every creature for a specific purpose.

Poisonous snakes have special **glands** similar to our **salivary glands**. These glands produce **venom** to poison their prey. Venom even helps them **digest** their food. The fangs that dispense venom are hollow, like the **syringe** a doctor uses. If a fang breaks off, there's another one in the roof of the snake's mouth to replace it!

Poisonous snakes have ways to warn us that they are dangerous — like bright colors or rattles. Aren't you glad God made snakes so we can tell them apart?

WHAT WE LEARNED

1 **List some ways that poisonous and non-poisonous snakes are different. What are some ways you can tell them apart?**

_____

_____

_____

_____

_____

_____

_____

2 **Describe the snake you created in Step 2. Now describe the snake you created in Step 3.**

_____

_____

_____

_____

_____

_____

_____

3 How were the two snakes you made similar? How were they different?

_____

_____

_____

_____

_____

_____

4 Using what you learned in Step 4, describe how poisonous snakes inject venom into their prey.

_____

_____

_____

_____

_____

_____

5 Why are snakes an important part of the environment?

_____

_____

_____

_____

_____

_____

! CONCLUSION

God made every creature for a specific purpose. Both poisonous and non-poisonous snakes play an important role in the environment. The characteristics of snakes can help us tell them apart.

FOOD FOR THOUGHT

Numbers 21:6-9 The people of Isreal were surrounded by poisionous snakes! Scripture tells us that God told Moses to put a bronze snake on a pole. Everyone who was bitten by a poisonous snake was saved by looking at the snake on the pole. By following God's instructions the people showed their trust in his saving power.

In John 3:14-15, Jesus talked about how he would be put on a pole, too (the cross), and those who looked to him would live! Jesus saved us through his death and resurrection. Like the people surrounded by poisonous snakes, we must look to Jesus and trust in God's saving power.

JOURNAL My Science Notes

_____

_____

_____

_____

_____

_____

_____

_____

_____

_____

_____

_____

_____

_____

_____

_____

_____

NAME _____

DUCK'S BACK

LESSON 3

FOCUS Animal Characteristics

OBJECTIVE To explore how a bird's feathers repel water

OVERVIEW It's starting to rain! Notice that ducks and geese don't seem to mind at all. Why don't they get soaked to the skin like we do? Let's explore what "water off a duck's back" means.

WHAT TO DO

STEP 1

Carefully **examine** the two pieces of cloth. **Describe** them in your journal.

STEP 2

Place one cloth on your work surface. Use your pipette to **squirt** some water onto it. **Watch** closely and **record** the results.

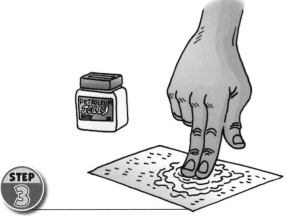

STEP 3

Place the other cloth on your work surface. **Coat** it with a layer of petroleum jelly. (Rub the jelly in thoroughly.) **Predict** what will happen when water is squirted onto this cloth. **Record** your predicition.

STEP 4

Use your pipette to **squirt** some water onto the treated cloth. **Watch** closely and **record** the results. Now **review** each step in this activity. **Share** and **compare** observations with your research team.

WHAT HAPPENED?

Birds have a **gland** that produces a special type of oil. Using their beaks, they rub this oil vigorously all over themselves, covering their feathers with a light, **protective coating**. (We used a thin layer of petroleum jelly on cloth to simulate this.) Without this protective oil, the cold rain and water would soak the bird, causing it to die.

But how does oil cause water to run off something? Usually, water **molecules** act just like little magnets. They tend to stick to most surfaces; sometimes they're **absorbed**. This makes the object very wet!

But water molecules just won't stick to oil. When they hit a bird's feathers, the light, oily coating prevents them from sticking, so they simply roll off — just like the water drops rolled off your cloth.

WHAT WE LEARNED

1 In Step 2, what happened to the piece of cloth when you poured water on it? Why do you think this happened?

_____

_____

_____

_____

_____

_____

2 What was your prediction in Step 3?
Why did you think this was what would happen?

_____

_____

_____

_____

_____

_____

_____

3 In Step 4, what happened to the piece of cloth when you poured water on it? Why do you think this happened?

_____

_____

_____

_____

_____

_____

4 How does oil cause water to run off something?

_____

_____

_____

_____

_____

_____

5 Pretend the two cloths are birds. Which one has a better chance of surviving in a very cold lake? Why?

_____

_____

_____

_____

_____

_____

CONCLUSION

Water molecules are attracted to each other, and to most other materials as well. A waterproof coating can help keep water molecules from sticking to the material's surface. When water molecules stick to each other, but not to the surface, they roll off easily.

FOOD FOR THOUGHT

Ephesians 6:10-11 As we've seen, birds keep themselves safe by putting on a protective coating. But each of us needs a protective coating, too! Satan's evil can soak into our souls just like water soaking into an unprotected cloth.

But Scripture offers us a unique form of protection. It tells us to put on the "armor of God." By reading, studying, and praying, we can learn to trust God better, adding a special protective coating to our lives.

Then when evil comes, it will roll away — just like water off a duck's back!

JOURNAL My Science Notes

_____

_____

_____

_____

_____

_____

_____

_____

_____

_____

_____

_____

_____

_____

_____

_____

_____

_____

LESSON 4

BUG OUT

FOCUS Ecosystems

OBJECTIVE To explore the predator/prey relationship

OVERVIEW Finding food is serious business for wild animals. If they don't find, catch, and consume enough food, they die! There's only so much food to go around. Competition for survival can be fierce. See if your predator can survive!

WHAT TO DO

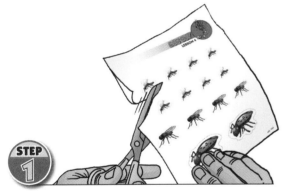

STEP 1

Find the "Bug Out" page in the back of your worktext (page 165). Carefully **cut out** all the bugs. Now **gather** all your team's bugs and **sort** them according to size. **Examine** the bugs carefully. **Record** your observations.

STEP 2

Scatter the bugs around your work surface. **Remove** the sticky-tongued "predator" from its container. **Examine** it carefully. Now you're ready to play "Bug Out"!

STEP 3

Take turns using the predator to catch bugs (two tries per turn). **Continue** until everyone on your team has had three turns. **Add** the numbers on the back of the bugs you caught to discover how much "food" your predator ate. **Record** the results.

STEP 4

Check your score. If your predator scored 6 food points or more, it survived! **Share** and **compare** observations with your research team. **Make notes** about how each team member's points were compiled.

?WHAT HAPPENED?

Any creature that catches and eats another is called a **predator**. Examples of predators include lions, hawks, snakes — even house cats when they're hunting outdoors! Any creature caught and eaten is **prey**. Most plant-eating animals are prey, including rabbits, deer, and mice. But predators can also become prey themselves! A hawk may catch a snake who caught a mouse, making the snake both predator and prey.

The game "Bug Out" simulates a predator's **environment**. Notice that you didn't catch a bug every time. That's life as a predator. Your lunch doesn't want to **be** your lunch!

The predator/prey relationship needs to be **balanced**. With too few predators, prey populations grow out of control, leading to death and starvation. Too many predators, and there's not enough prey to go around.

?WHAT WE LEARNED

1 How were the "prey" creatures you cut out in Step 1 similar? How were they different?

_____

_____

_____

_____

_____

_____

2 As a predator, which bugs did you try to catch first? Why? If you played this game again, how would you change your stategy?

_____

_____

_____

_____

_____

3 As you played the game, sometimes the predator missed. If you were a real predator, what would be the result of missing?

_____

_____

_____

_____

_____

_____

4 What would happen if the predators in an area caught all the prey?

_____

_____

_____

_____

_____

_____

5 What would happen to the prey in an area if the predators were all removed? What might happen over time?

_____

_____

_____

_____

_____

_____

CONCLUSION

Predators need to catch enough prey to survive. Failure to do this will result in death. In the long run, the numbers of predators and prey must remain in balance for both groups to survive and thrive.

FOOD FOR THOUGHT

Exodus 10:4-6 When the balance between predator and prey is disrupted, serious problems result. Scripture tells of a time when millions of locusts (like very hungry grasshoppers) swarmed over Egypt, devouring everything in sight!

When our lives get out of balance (for whatever reason), we tend to leave God out of the picture. We get too busy and don't spend enough time with God. But these distractions can "devour" us, just like the locusts devoured the Egyptians' food!

Keep your life in balance. Keep in touch with God!

JOURNAL My Science Notes

_____

_____

_____

_____

_____

_____

_____

_____

_____

_____

_____

_____

_____

_____

_____

_____

_____

_____

NAME _____

LEAF RUBBING

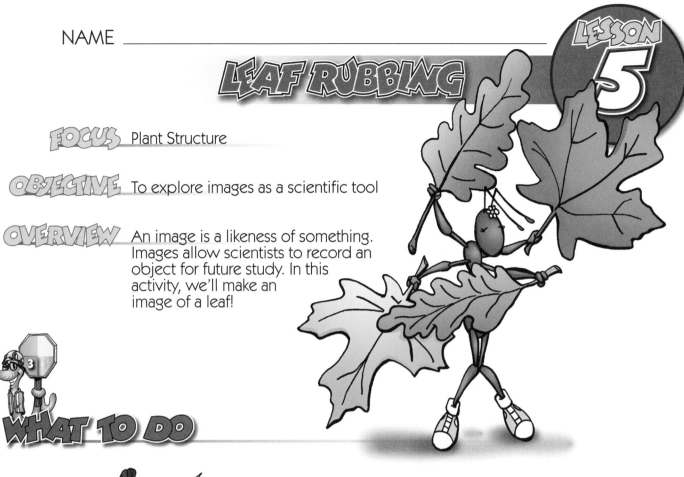

FOCUS Plant Structure

OBJECTIVE To explore images as a scientific tool

OVERVIEW An image is a likeness of something. Images allow scientists to record an object for future study. In this activity, we'll make an image of a leaf!

WHAT TO DO

STEP 1

Follow your teacher on a research expedition. Your goal is to **find** leaves with interesting shapes and easy-to-see structures. When you return to class, **examine** your leaves carefully. **Record** observations in your journal about the leaves you have collected.

STEP 2

Select an interesting leaf from your collection. **Lay** it on your work surface and **examine** it carefully. Now **make** a drawing of the leaf in your journal. Make notes comparing your drawing to the actual leaf.

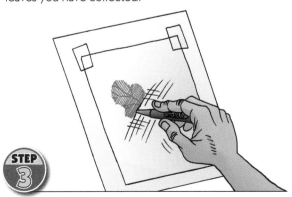

STEP 3

Lay a leaf in the center of a piece of paper, then **cover** it with the paper your teacher gives you. **Tape** both papers to keep them from moving. Now gently **rub** a crayon or pencil over the top sheet. **Cover** the entire leaf. **Observe** what happens to the paper and record the results.

STEP 4

The image you made in Step 3 is called a "rubbing." **Examine** your leaf rubbing carefully. **Compare** it with the drawing you made in Step 2. **Record** similarities and differences in the two images. **Share** and **compare** observations with your research team.

An **image** is a likeness or a picture of something. Scientists constantly make images of the things they study. Models, photographs, x-rays, drawings — all are examples of images that scientists use to increase their understanding.

Compare the detail of your leaf drawing (Step 2) to your leaf **rubbing** (Step 3). The drawing is a good outline, but the rubbing clearly shows many of the leaf's smaller structures. Those tiny parts have important jobs to do. For example, the **stem** and **veins** provide **support** for the leaf. They also **transport** materials through the leaf, similar to the way blood circulates through your body.

The better the image a scientist makes, the more they can learn from it!

WHAT WE LEARNED

1 **Describe a leaf you chose in Step 1. What are some of its most interesting features?**

_____

_____

_____

_____

_____

_____

_____

2 **Compare the drawing you made in Step 2 to the actual leaf. How is your drawing different from the real leaf?**

_____

_____

_____

_____

_____

_____

_____

3 Why was it important to use thin paper in Step 3? Describe what happened as you rubbed your pencil or crayon across the sheet.

_____

_____

_____

_____

_____

_____

4 Why are the stem and veins important parts of a leaf? Describe (or sketch) how the stem and veins are connected to the leaf.

_____

_____

_____

_____

_____

_____

5 Why is an image a useful tool in scientific study?

_____

_____

_____

_____

_____

_____

CONCLUSION

Images are useful tools in helping scientists learn more about living things. The image you made highlights some important parts of a leaf. Each of these parts has a specific job or function to carry out for the plant's benefit.

FOOD FOR THOUGHT

Genesis 1:27 The image you made was a kind of photocopy. You copied the shape of the leaf onto a piece of paper by rubbing it. In other words, you made an image of the leaf using the real thing.

Scripture tells us that God created us in His image. When you look at a leaf rubbing, you think about the tree it came from. When you look in a mirror, you should think about where **you** came from! You are created in the image of God. Just like the leaves of trees are different, each special in its own way, so each of us is special just as God made us! And when people look at us, they should see the character of God!

JOURNAL My Science Notes

NAME _____

FRUIT SPONGE

FOCUS Food Preservation

OBJECTIVE To explore how water affects spoilage

OVERVIEW If you leave most foods out of the refrigerator, they spoil. But dried fruit doesn't spoil. Why not? This activity will help you discover some facts about preserving food.

WHAT TO DO

STEP 1

Carefully **examine** all the materials used in this activity—containers, grapes, and raisins. **Discuss** similarities and differences between grapes and raisins. **Record** observations in your journal.

STEP 2

Using masking tape and a marker, **label** each container. **Place** five grapes in container 1. **Place** five raisins in container 2. **Fill** container 3 half full of water, then **add** five raisins. Finish by putting the lids on all three containers.

STEP 3

Place the containers where your teacher directs. Carefully **examine** all three containers every day, taking care not to disturb the contents. In your journal, **make detailed notes** about what you see. (Headings like "Day 1," "Day 2," etc. will help organize your notes.)

STEP 4

After making notes on the final day, **discard** the contents of all containers. **Wash** and **dry** them, and return them to your teacher. Now **review** your notes. **Share** and **compare** observations with your research team.

WHAT HAPPENED?

All living things are made of tiny structures called **cells**. Cells are surrounded by a tough covering called a **membrane**. The membrane controls what gets into and out of the cell. Food and oxygen need to get in, and waste products need to get out.

The membrane also **regulates** the amount of water in the cell through a process called **osmosis**. When fruit is **dehydrated** (dried out), the membrane releases the water inside the cells to the dry air outside the cells. The **bacteria** and other organisms that cause spoilage need water to live. The less water they have available, the longer it takes for the item to **decompose**.

The reverse is also true. When you put raisins (dried grapes) in water, some water goes back through the cell membranes, and the fruit looks a lot like it did before dehydration! With the water back, the **rehydrated** raisins will now spoil quickly.

WHAT WE LEARNED

1 Compare the raisins and grapes you used in Step 1. How were they similar? How were they different?

_____

_____

_____

_____

_____

_____

_____

2 Describe the raisins and grapes when you completed Step 2. What did they look like?

_____

_____

_____

_____

_____

_____

_____

3 Describe the raisins and grapes after Step 3 was completed. What did they look like?

_____

_____

_____

_____

_____

_____

4 Based on what you've learned, how are grapes made into raisins? Why does it take raisins longer to spoil than grapes?

_____

_____

_____

_____

_____

_____

5 If you left the raisins in the water for several more days, what would have happened? Why?

_____

_____

_____

_____

_____

_____

CONCLUSION

In order for something to decompose (spoil), there must be adequate water available. When we dehydrate food, we preserve it by removing life-giving water from bacteria and other organisms that spoil food. In other words, drier foods don't spoil as quickly.

FOOD FOR THOUGHT

Luke 6:43-45 Just as we preserve fruit by removing excess water, sometimes God must "preserve" us by removing things in our lives that cause us to be "spoiled." Our job is to study and pray, seeking to know God better and trusting in the plan he has for our lives.

Scripture tells us that "every tree is known by its fruit." You don't find apples growing on an orange tree, or blueberries on a grape vine! The same is true of people. The way that we treat others shows a lot about what kind of person we are inside. And our kindness to others should be a reflection of the loving God we serve.

JOURNAL My Science Notes

NAME _____

TOUCH TESTER

FOCUS Body Function

OBJECTIVE To explore the sense of touch

OVERVIEW When we talk about senses, we often think of sight, smell, or hearing. Your sense of touch is very important, too! In this activity, we'll explore how our skin acts as a touch sensor.

WHAT TO DO

STEP 1

With your research team, **discuss** the following five skin areas: fingertip, palm of hand, back of hand, back of arm, shoulder. **Predict** which of these areas are the most sensitive and which are the least. (It's okay to disagree). **Record** your predictions.

STEP 2

Push one pin into the cork's side. **Push** two pins in one end of the cork, about 1/4" inch apart. **Push** three pins in the other end of the cork, in a straight line about 1/4" inch apart. (Be sure the pins are secure and exactly the same distance from the surface.).

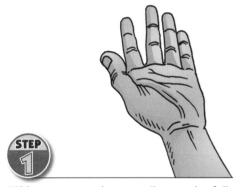

STEP 3

Ask one team member to sit down. **Blindfold** him/her carefully. To start your test, gently **touch** a skin area with one of the pin combinations. Use any order and pin combination you choose. Each time you touch **ask**, "How many pins are there?" **Record** the guesses.

STEP 4

Continue testing until you have checked all five areas. **Trade** places and **repeat** Step 3. Once every team member has had a turn, **review** your test results. (Note: pins and numbers guessed may not always agree!) Now **share** and **compare** observations.

WHAT HAPPENED?

Touch is one of the **five senses** of the body — and a very important one, too! Without the sense of touch, we would have no warning of heat, pressure, cold, or other potential dangers. Our bodies could be damaged before our brains even knew there was a problem!

God designed our bodies so that the skin has **sensitivity**. This sensitivity helps your brain gather information, process it, and react quickly.

Notice that the number of **pressure receptors** (a special kind of **neuron**, or nerve cell), is different depending on what part of the body is touched. Although we only used the hand in this activity, we were able to identify areas on the skin where the number of these neurons varied significantly.

WHAT WE LEARNED

1 List the five skin areas from Step 1. What were your predictions regarding sensitivity for each of these?

_____

_____

_____

_____

_____

_____

2 In Step 2, why was it critical to make sure all the pins were exactly the same height?

_____

_____

_____

_____

_____

_____

3 In Step 3, why was it important to blindfold the person being tested? What sense did the blindfold eliminate?

_____

_____

_____

_____

_____

4 Based on your test results, what area of the skin appeared to be the least sensitive? Why?

_____

_____

_____

_____

_____

5 Based on your test results, what area of the skin appeared to be the most sensitive? Why is sensitivity so important here?

_____

_____

_____

_____

_____

_____

CONCLUSION

The skin is a very important sense organ. Its sensitivity helps protect our bodies from harm. The number of touch receptors can vary significantly depending on what part of the body is involved.

FOOD FOR THOUGHT

Job 10:11-12 This Scripture talks about how God created our skin and flesh, and of God's constant care. Your skin is a marvelous creation. Look at all it does for you! In many ways, your safety and health depend on the sensitivity of your skin.

Just as our skin's sensitivity helps keep us safe from physical harm, so our sensitivity to God and obedience to his Word helps keep us safe from spiritual harm. Reading God's Word will help that sensitivity grow.

Spend time this week getting to know God better!

JOURNAL My Science Notes

_____
_____
_____
_____
_____
_____
_____
_____
_____
_____
_____
_____
_____
_____
_____
_____
_____

NAME _____

RAPID REACTION

FOCUS Body Function

OBJECTIVE To explore the nervous system

OVERVIEW Our brains process a lot of information. Our hands do many practical things. Can the brain and hands work together? This activity explores what happens when these two body parts try to function simultaneously.

WHAT TO DO

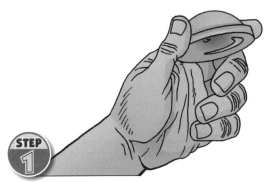

STEP 1

Carefully **examine** your popper. Turn it inside out and place it on your work surface, flat side down. Now **watch** the popper. Be patient! After something happens, **record** what you observed and why you think it happened.

STEP 2

Retrieve the popper. **Stand** facing it with your hands behind your back. **Ask** a team member to "reset" the popper. Now **watch** closely. When the popper jumps, try to grab it before it hits the table. **Repeat** this three times. **Record** the results.

STEP 3

Ask a team member to reset the popper. **Stand** with your back to it, hands at your sides. When you hear it "pop," **turn** quickly and try to grab the popper. **Repeat** three times. **Record** the results.

STEP 4

Review each step in the activity. **Record** what you observed. **Share** and **compare** observations with your research team.

WHAT HAPPENED?

Complex living creatures have complex **nervous systems**. God designed humans with a marvelous system that includes the **brain**, the **spinal cord**, and the **nerves** connected to the rest of the body.

We tested this marvelous system in this lesson. First, your eyes saw the popper jump. This information went to the brain, which said "grab it!" That sent a signal to the muscles, which moved, making adjustments according to additional information sent to the brain by the eyes. In Step 3, we made the process even more complex by using the ears to start the action!

The time it took to respond is called the **reaction time**. Remember, reaction times will vary from person to person since each of our nervous systems is slightly different.

WHAT WE LEARNED

1 **To begin Step 1, the popper was turned inside out. What happened when it was released?**

_____

_____

_____

_____

_____

_____

2 **In step 2, what eventually happened as you waited? Why do you think this happened?**

_____

_____

_____

_____

_____

_____

3 Describe the steps your nervous system had to complete in order for you to react and grab the popper in Step 2.

_____

_____

_____

_____

_____

_____

4 Compare the reactions required in Step 2 with the reactions required in Step 3. How were they similar? How were they different?

_____

_____

_____

_____

_____

_____

5 Using what you've learned in this activity, tell why you think some medications say "Do not take before driving."

_____

_____

_____

_____

_____

_____

! CONCLUSION

God designed the human body with a marvelous nervous system. It helps us gather information, process that information, make appropriate decisions, and then act on those decisions. Since everyone's nervous system is different, the process will often take different amounts of time for different people.

FOOD FOR THOUGHT

Isaiah 1:16-17 Through regular, daily practice, a person can train their nervous system to do many things well. Music, art, and sports are just a few examples.

In this Scripture, God is encouraging us to stop doing wrong things, and to start learning to do right things. This is good counsel — not only for students, but also for parents and teachers!

Our marvelous nervous system can help. Just like practicing music, art, and sports, the more we do the right things, the easier and more natural they will become!

JOURNAL My Science Notes

LESSON 9

BONE BUILDING

FOCUS Body Structure

OBJECTIVE To explore major bones of the body

OVERVIEW Just as a tall building needs support, our bodies need a strong framework in order to function. In this activity, we'll explore some of the major parts of our support system.

WHAT TO DO

STEP 1

Remove the "Bone Building" page from the back of your worktext (page 167). **Examine** it carefully. **Record** your observations. There are similar bones inside of you — only yours are covered with muscle, blood vessels, skin, and hair!

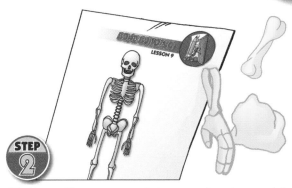

STEP 2

Working with your research team, **make** clay models of each bone. Keep them about the same size as the picture. Once every team member has made at least one bone, and all bones are accounted for, **examine** the results. **Record** your observations.

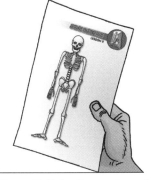

STEP 3

Cut a sheet of paper and **insert** it in the box lid. Now carefully **place** the bones you made onto the paper one at a time. **Ask** one team member to watch the "Bone Building" page to make sure you're putting them in the right order and location.

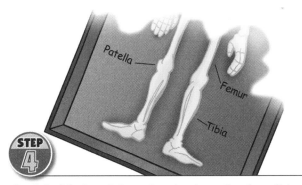

STEP 4

Carefully **label** each bone by drawing a line from it to a blank spot on the paper. **Write** the name of the bone at the end of the line. **Review** each step in this activity. **Share** and **compare** observations with your research team.

WHAT HAPPENED?

Imagine trying to carry water without a bucket . . . or building a large paper kite without a frame . . . or baking a cake without a pan. It's just as hard to imagine a body without any bones!

Your skeletal system provides more than just a structural support for your body. **Bones** also form a "cage" to protect your **vital organs** (heart, lungs, etc.). Bones store important **minerals** that the body needs (like calcium). Bones produce **blood cells** (red and white). Bones especially work with **muscles** to allow movement.

In addition to bones, our **skeletal system** contains other important parts. **Ligaments** hold the bones together at the **joints**. **Tendons** attach muscles to the bones, allowing these muscles to pull the bones, creating movement.

WHAT WE LEARNED

1 **How is our skeletal system similar to the framework of a building? How is it different?**

_____

_____

_____

_____

_____

_____

_____

2 **Describe the shape of at least two bones you created in Step 2.**

_____

_____

_____

_____

_____

_____

_____

3 Based on your research, what part of the skeleton contains the largest number of bones? Which bone is the longest?

_____

_____

_____

_____

_____

_____

4 In addition to bones, what are some other parts of the skeletal system? What do these parts do?

_____

_____

_____

_____

_____

_____

5 In addition to providing structural support for the body, what are some other functions of bones?

_____

_____

_____

_____

_____

_____

_____

! CONCLUSION

Your skeletal system plays an important role in keeping your body healthy and strong. In addition to structural support, bones serve many other functions.

FOOD FOR THOUGHT

Romans 12:4-5 The skeletal system provides strong structural support for the body, but it also has many other important functions — storing key minerals, building blood cells, and protecting vital organs like the heart.

Scripture tells us we're all members of God's body, but God has given each of us different functions. You may be an effective organizer, a friendly hostess, or an accurate record keeper. You may have the gift of being a good speaker, an efficient helper, or a kind, encouraging friend. Regardless of your gift, strive to be a good "bone" and support the body!

JOURNAL My Science Notes

Forces

LESSONS 10-18

Forces

In this section you'll discover how "push and pull" form the basis for all physical movement. You'll explore simple machines (levers, pulleys). You'll work with Newton's laws of motion. You'll even learn to understand concepts like torque, inertia, and buoyancy.

NAME _____

FREAKY FROST

FOCUS Crystals

OBJECTIVE To explore changes in matter and the forces that cause them

OVERVIEW Our world is filled with matter in various forms. For matter to change forms, some kind of force is required. In this activity, we'll take a closer look at one way that a change can take place.

WHAT TO DO

STEP 1

Open the bottle of magnesium sulfate and **set** the lid on your work surface. Carefully **fill** the lid with magnesium sulfate. **Observe** the materials and **record** your observations. Now **fill** a paper cup one-third full of warm water and **set** it on your work surface.

STEP 2

Pour the magnesium sulfate into the water. **Stir** the solution with a craft stick. Most of the magnesium sulfate should dissolve, but not all of it. (If it all dissolves, add a little bit more.) **Stop** stirring and **observe** the solution in the cup. **Record** what you see.

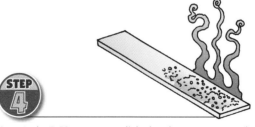

STEP 3

Dip one end of a microscope slide into the solution. (Make sure half the slide is thoroughly covered.) **Move** your slide to the area your teacher indicates. **Record** your observations. **Clean up** as directed by your teacher.

STEP 4

[next day] **Place** your slide back on your work surface. **Observe** it carefully. **Record** what you see. Carefully **review** each step in this activity. **Share** and **compare** observations with your research team.

Matter has three basic forms: **solid**, **liquid**, and **gas**. Changes in matter (at least here on Earth) always involve switching from one of these **three states** to another.

But **force** is required for a change in matter. In this case, stirring (push/pull force) helped the water **dissolve** the chemical, turning a solid into a liquid and forming a **solution**. Drying the slide (heat force) made the water **evaporate**, forming a gas. The rest of the solution remained on the slide, turning back into a solid.

So, the **Tabletop Frost** you made wasn't really frost. It was tiny **crystals** of magnesium sulfate — the same chemical you stirred into the water! (Crystals are small, well organized pieces of certain types of solids.) The crystals were simply left behind when the water evaporated from the solution.

WHAT WE LEARNED

1 Describe the water you used in Step 1. What state of matter was it? How did the water look after you completed Step 2?

_____

_____

_____

_____

_____

_____

_____

2 Describe the magnesium sulfate. What state of matter was it? How did the magnesium sulfate look after you completed Step 2?

_____

_____

_____

_____

_____

_____

_____

3 Describe the slide you used in Step 3. What state of matter was it?

_____

_____

_____

_____

_____

_____

4 Describe the "frost" that appeared after Step 4. What state of matter was it? How was it different from the magnesium sulfate in Step 2?

_____

_____

_____

_____

_____

_____

5 Name some of the forces involved in this activity.
Tell how each one was used.

_____

_____

_____

_____

_____

_____

_____

CONCLUSION

The three states of matter are solid, liquid, and gas. In order for changes to take place in matter, some kind of force must be involved.

FOOD FOR THOUGHT

John 3:3 Matter can't change from one state to another without some kind of force being involved. Forces can be powerful agents for change.

Like matter, people really don't change much unless there's some powerful force involved. We tend to be selfish and unkind. Sometimes we hurt each other's feelings. We go on our foolish way — until we encounter the power of God's love!

Jesus said unless we're "born again" (completely changed) we can't enter God's kingdom. He wants us to experience God's life-changing power.

JOURNAL My Science Notes

_____

_____

_____

_____

_____

_____

_____

_____

_____

_____

_____

_____

_____

_____

_____

_____

_____

_____

NAME _____

BERRY BOAT

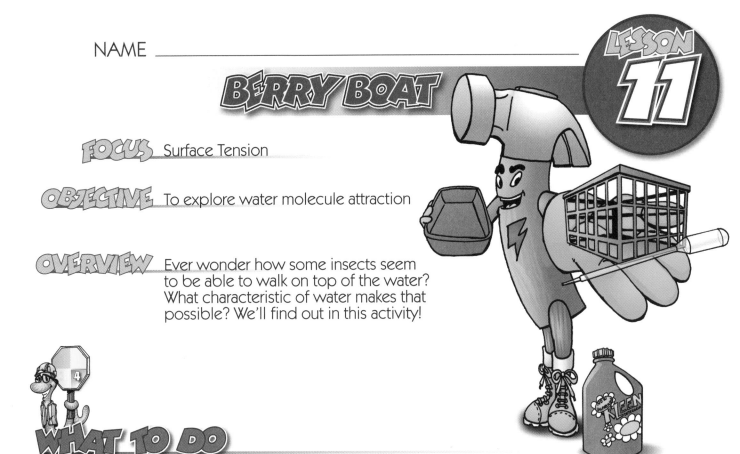

FOCUS Surface Tension

OBJECTIVE To explore water molecule attraction

OVERVIEW Ever wonder how some insects seem to be able to walk on top of the water? What characteristic of water makes that possible? We'll find out in this activity!

WHAT TO DO

STEP 1

Fill an aluminum pie plate with water. Gently **place** the berry box on the water's surface so that it floats. (This may take several tries.) **Observe** the floating box and **make notes** about what you see — especially between the squares in the bottom of the box.

STEP 2

Fill a pipette with water. Gently **add** one drop to the water's surface near the box. **Record** the results. (Make sure everyone on your research team gets a turn.)

STEP 3

Dip a toothpick into liquid detergent. Using the toothpick, **transfer** one drop of detergent to the water's surface near the box. If nothing happens, **add** another drop or two. **Record** the results.

STEP 4

Carefully **review** each step in this activity, checking the notes you made. **Share** and **compare** observations with your research team.

WHAT HAPPENED?

If you looked closely in Step 1, you could see the effects of **gravity** trying to pull your **Berry Boat** down! This caused raised "dimples" of water between the squares on the box's bottom.

The box didn't sink because the water **molecules** on the surface were attracting each other and forming a kind of skin called **surface tension**. Surface tension is what allows some insects to walk or skate on the top of a pond. If you placed your **Berry Boat** carefully, the surface tension was just enough to keep it floating, thus defeating gravity.

In Step 3, you added a little detergent. Detergent broke the surface tension by not letting the water molecules stick to each other. Without the strong surface tension, your **Berry Boat** had to give in to the force of gravity. In other words, it sank!

WHAT WE LEARNED

1 **Review Step 1. Describe the surface of the water between the squares in the bottom of the Berry Boat. What caused this?**

_____

_____

_____

_____

_____

_____

_____

2 **What made the Berry Boat float in spite of gravity trying to pull it to the bottom? Why did adding water in Step 2 have no effect?**

_____

_____

_____

_____

_____

_____

3 Describe what happened in Step 3 when you added the detergent.

_____

_____

_____

_____

_____

_____

4 Two things were necessary for the Berry Boat to sink.
What force was involved? What was the other factor?

_____

_____

_____

_____

_____

_____

5 If you repeated this activity using a small piece of wood, what would
be the result of Step 3? What makes this example different?

_____

_____

_____

_____

_____

_____

CONCLUSION

Matter and forces go hand in hand. There are forces that cause matter to behave in certain ways. (Surface tension is a good example of this.) If these forces are changed, matter is affected. (Breaking surface tension with detergent is an example.)

FOOD FOR THOUGHT

Matthew 14:25 You may have been surprised to see the Berry Boat float. That's because you didn't fully understand the forces involved. But can you imagine how surprised the disciples were to see Jesus walking on the water! They didn't understand the forces involved there, either.

In science, we study the results of forces God created. But we must never forget that the ultimate Force behind these forces is God. Scripture tells us that the winds and waves obeyed his will. Even unthinking water and air knew to follow God's commands! Shouldn't we seek to know and follow God's will even more?

JOURNAL My Science Notes

_____
_____
_____
_____
_____
_____
_____
_____
_____
_____
_____
_____
_____
_____
_____
_____
_____

NAME _____

BORROWED AIR

FOCUS Air Pressure

OBJECTIVE To explore air as a form of matter

OVERVIEW As we learned in Lesson 10, matter has three basic states: solid, liquid, and gas. But state is only one characteristic of matter. In this activity, we'll look at another important characteristic.

WHAT TO DO

STEP 1

Fill a large, deep bowl with water. **Set** two small clear plastic cups beside it. **Examine** these materials closely and **record** your observations.

STEP 2

Lower one cup into the bowl, filling it with water. **Hold** the cup completely underwater and **flip** it upside down. Now **hold** the other cup upside down and **push** it straight down into the bowl, making sure the cup stays full of air. **Record** your observations.

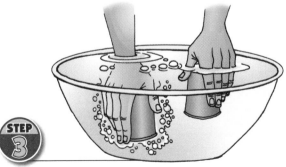

STEP 3

Move the first cup (full of water) so its opening is beside and slightly above the second cup (full of air). **Tilt** the second cup and **pour** the air upwards into the first cup. If you miss, repeat Steps 2 and 3. **Record** your observations.

STEP 4

When every team member has had a turn, **empty** the water and **clean up** any mess. **Review** each step in this activity and **record** what you've seen. Now **share** and **compare** observations with your research team.

WHAT HAPPENED?

Any material (**solid**, **liquid**, or **gas**) is called matter. All matter has something called **density**. Density refers to the amount of matter in a given **volume** of space. Both cups had the same volume, right? But if you fill one with water and the other with air, which weighs more? The water, of course! This tells us water is more **dense** than air.

Density is what makes this activity work. Because air is **less** dense than water, you can "pour" it upwards from one cup to the other. A cork held underwater would also go up since it's less dense than water, too.

Both the cork and the air are lighter than the same volume of water. So while gravity is pulling them straight down, the heavier water is pushing in the opposite direction — and pushing much harder! As a result, up they go!

WHAT WE LEARNED

1 List some examples of solids, liquids, and gasses that you used or observed in this activity.

_____

_____

_____

_____

_____

_____

2 Why were you able to "pour" the air upward? What forces were involved in this process?

_____

_____

_____

_____

_____

_____

3 Compare the first cup in Step 3 to the second cup. How were they similar? How were they different?

_____

_____

_____

_____

_____

_____

4 You have two cups full of different materials. Explain one way you can compare the density of matter in these cups.

_____

_____

_____

_____

_____

_____

5 A scuba diver loses his light in a dark area underwater. He can't tell which way is up. How can his air bubbles help him find the surface?

_____

_____

_____

_____

_____

_____

CONCLUSION

Materials with the same volume can have different densities. The density of matter can have an impact on how it behaves. Different forms of matter (like water and air) can interact, but some sort of force is required for this to happen.

FOOD FOR THOUGHT

John 8:32 In this week's activity, the air was trapped inside the cup. It couldn't get out. The water was trapped in a cup, too. Even though there were two different cups and the air and water were very different forms of matter, both were completely trapped until an outside force set them free.

Sometimes we're trapped in situations where there seems to be no hope. It may be something bad that we did, or it may be the result of something someone else has done. But Jesus has promised that "the truth will set you free!" We have a way out of the trap, and it comes from trusting God.

JOURNAL My Science Notes

NAME _____

GRAVITY GONE

FOCUS Gravity

OBJECTIVE To explore how gravity works

OVERVIEW Gravity is a force that affects everything, and it can be found everywhere in the universe (at least, as far as we know). Yet this activity appears to defy gravity. See if you can figure out what's happening here.

WHAT TO DO

STEP 1

Place the rubber ball in the jar. **Replace** the lid and **tighten** firmly. Gently **shake** the jar back and forth (not up and down!). **Observe** what happens and **make notes** about what you see.

STEP 2

Open the jar and **remove** the ball. **Fill** the jar half full of uncooked rice. **Replace** the lid and **tighten** firmly. Gently **shake** the jar back and forth. **Observe** what happens and **make notes** about what you see.

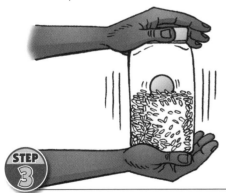

STEP 3

Open the jar and **place** the rubber ball on top of the rice. **Replace** the lid and **tighten** firmly. **Shake** the jar back and forth. **Observe** what happens and **make notes** about the position of the ball and the rice.

STEP 4

Turn the jar upside down quickly. **Record** the ball's position. **Predict** what might happen if you shake the jar again. **Shake** the jar again. **Observe** what happens to the ball. Now **review** each step in this activity. **Share** and **compare** observations with your research team.

Of course, there's no such thing as an **anti-gravity machine** . . . at least not on this scale! Yet the ball appeared like magic, rising to the top. How did that happen?

Put your hand on your desk and push down hard. Nothing happens, does it? The **molecules** in your very solid hand can't go through the desk. The desk can't go through your hand, either. The desk molecules simply push right back.

When you jiggled the jar back and forth, the rice obeyed the **law of gravity** and began to settle, just like the ball. But the rice grains were much smaller than the rubber ball. Because of their size, the rice grains kept slipping under the ball and pushing it up. Instead of going down, the jiggling ball just went round and round— and up!

WHAT WE LEARNED

1 **Describe what happened to the ball in Step 1. What forces were acting on the ball?**

_____

_____

_____

_____

_____

_____

_____

2 **Describe what happened to the rice in step 2. What forces were acting on the rice?**

_____

_____

_____

_____

_____

_____

_____

3 Describe what happened to the ball in step 3.
What forces were acting on the ball and the rice?

_____

_____

_____

_____

_____

_____

4 What was your prediction? Describe what happened to the ball
in step 4. What force was acting on the ball and rice?

_____

_____

_____

_____

_____

_____

5 Describe why the ball seemed to disobey the law of gravity in Step 4.

_____

_____

_____

_____

_____

_____

CONCLUSION

Sometimes matter behaves in ways that seem to defy logic. But when we understand what's going on, it makes sense again. Gravity is a particular type of force that affects everything in the known universe.

FOOD FOR THOUGHT

1 Corinthians 10:13 Gravity affects everything and everybody! In this activity, it seemed impossible for the ball to pop out on top of the rice. But once we understood what was going on, it all made sense again.

Scripture tells us that sin affects everything and everyone, too. No one is immune. Because of sin, things sometimes look impossible, like there's no way out.

Remember — nothing is impossible with God! He's always ready to help us. And as we learn more about God, many "impossible" things begin to make sense.

JOURNAL My Science Notes

_____

_____

_____

_____

_____

_____

_____

_____

_____

_____

_____

_____

_____

_____

_____

_____

_____

_____

NAME _____

CATCHING COINS

FOCUS Inertia

OBJECTIVE To explore inertia and movement

OVERVIEW To move something, you have to supply force (either push or pull). Gravity is one force that moves things. In this activity, we'll explore gravity and a property of matter called inertia.

WHAT TO DO

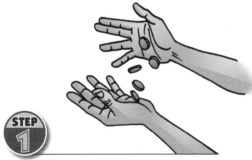

STEP 1

Stack five pennies on top of each other. **Lift** them with one hand. **Place** your other hand about six inches below the held coins. Let them go and **catch** them with the hand beneath. **Record** the results.

STEP 2

Hold your arm like the illustration above. **Practice** jerking your elbow straight down as the palm of your hand comes up, over, and down. **Practice** several times to get the feel of it. **Observe** your team members as they practice and make suggestions if asked.

STEP 3

Repeat Step 2, only this time try it with a penny on your elbow. Try to **catch** the penny before it falls. (Make sure no one is in front of you when you do this!) Once you're successful, try it with two pennies, then three. After a few tries, **record** your observations.

STEP 4

Carefully **review** each step in this activity, checking the notes you made. Now **share** and **compare** observations with your research team.

WHAT HAPPENED?

Inertia is Newton's first law of motion, and an important **property** of **matter**. This law states that an object won't move until a **force** is applied. (Remember, a force is always either a **push** or a **pull**.)

The law of inertia also states that if something is already moving, it will continue moving until another force is applied to stop or change its direction. Using the brakes to stop your bike is a good example of a force interrupting inertia.

Inertia is what held the pennies motionless on your arm. When you suddenly dropped your arm straight down, there was a split second before the force of **gravity** got the pennies moving very fast. This momentary delay allowed your rapidly moving hand to snatch the pennies right out of space.

WHAT WE LEARNED

1 What was the force discussed in this activity?
What property of matter had an impact on this force? Why?

_____

_____

_____

_____

_____

_____

_____

2 Describe what happened in Step 1.
What force was demonstrated in this step?

_____

_____

_____

_____

_____

_____

_____

3 Describe Step 2. Why was it important to practice this movement?

_____

_____

_____

_____

_____

_____

4 Why did you have to move your elbow down in order to catch the coins? What property of matter helped you catch the coins?

_____

_____

_____

_____

_____

_____

5 What would have happened if you moved your arm slower in Step 3? How would inertia have affected the coins?

_____

_____

_____

_____

_____

_____

_____

CONCLUSION

The law of inertia states that if an object is not moving, it will remain motionless until a force strong enough to move it is applied. A moving object will continue to move until a force strong enough to stop or redirect it is encountered.

FOOD FOR THOUGHT

Mark 10:13-16 Imagine for a moment that you are a penny on someone's arm, all alone and helpless, ready to be launched into space! Far up in the air, doom is bearing down on you. Suddenly, your world falls away . . .

Then the next instant a warm and comforting hand grabs you right out of space, snatching you to safety! How do you think you would feel?

Scripture tells about Jesus' great love for us. Whenever you feel lonely and lost, he's always there, ready to comfort and protect you.

JOURNAL My Science Notes

_____
_____
_____
_____
_____
_____
_____
_____
_____
_____
_____
_____
_____
_____
_____
_____
_____

MONKEY BUSINESS

LESSON 15

FOCUS Torque

OBJECTIVE To explore how torque can change the direction of force

OVERVIEW We've learned that forces are needed to move something. But how can a force traveling in one direction make something move in the opposite direction? In this activity, we'll find out!

WHAT TO DO

STEP 1

Find the "Monkey Business" page in the back of your work-text (page 169). Carefully **cut** out your monkey. Now **cut** two one-inch pieces off a soda straw. **Place** the monkey and the straw pieces on your work surface.

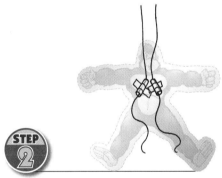

STEP 2

Firmly **tape** the two soda straws to the back of your monkey (see illustration). **Cut** a piece of string about five feet long, then **thread** the ends through the top of the straws. **Leave** about six inches of string below each straw. **Examine** your work and **make notes** about what you see.

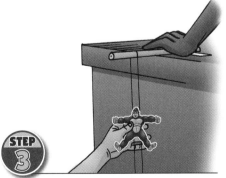

STEP 3

Ask a team member to hold a pencil with one end sticking off the work surface. **Place** the looped end of the string over the pencil and let the monkey hang below. **Even** the loose ends of the string and **level** your monkey. **Predict** what might happen if you pull gently on the string.

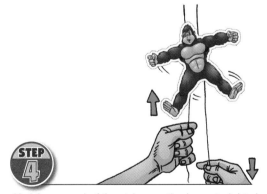

STEP 4

Hold one end of the string motionless, straight down from the monkey. Gently **pull** straight down on the other string. Now **hold** this string still and gently **pull** the other one. **Repeat** and **observe** the monkey's movements. **Share** and **compare** observations with your research team.

WHAT HAPPENED?

Forces make things move. Forces wash your clothes, move your bike, pump your blood, play your stereo, fill your water glass – the list goes on and on. Without forces, you'd sit in one spot forever with nothing to do, watch, or listen to. Actually, without forces working in your body, you wouldn't even be alive!

Torque is a turning or twisting force. Sometimes it behaves in ways we don't immediately understand. You pulled **down** on the string, but the monkey climbed **up**! How? Notice the two straws on the back of the monkey were taped at an angle. When you pulled the string, it wanted to go straight down. But it couldn't because the straw was at an angle. Instead, your downward pull created torque, causing the string to slightly twist in one direction. This made the monkey twist slightly too, and that twisting motion (torque) pulled the monkey up a little on that side.

WHAT WE LEARNED

1 **Why did the two straw pieces on the monkey's back need to be angled? What would have happened if they were straight?**

_____

_____

_____

_____

_____

_____

_____

2 **What did you predict in step 3? How did your prediction reflect what actually happened in Step 4?**

_____

_____

_____

_____

_____

_____

_____

3 Why did the monkey go **up** when you pulled **down** on the string?

4 Describe "torque." What kind of force is it?

5 Based on what you've learned about torque, give another example of a twisting force being transferred from one place to another.

CONCLUSION

Forces make things move. A twisting force is called torque. Forces can be transferred from one place to another.

FOOD FOR THOUGHT

Romans 12:9 You had to grasp the string tightly to apply the force (torque) needed for the monkey to climb. If you didn't hang on, then nothing would have happened.

Scripture tells us to hang on to what is good and let go of evil. For instance, we shouldn't just pretend to love others, we should **really** love them! Remember, all good things come from God: love, family, real friends, good health — all of the many blessings that surround us.

Be sure to hang on to the great things God has given you!

JOURNAL My Science Notes

_____

_____

_____

_____

_____

_____

_____

_____

_____

_____

_____

_____

_____

_____

_____

_____

NAME _____

FLOATING FIRE

FOCUS Buoyancy

OBJECTIVE To explore how things float

OVERVIEW Some things float. Some things don't. Since gravity is always trying to pull things down, why doesn't everything sink? We'll explore the answer in this activity.

WHAT TO DO

STEP 1

Pour water in the bottle until it's up to the rim. **Predict** what might happen to a pin dropped into the bottle. (Don't do it, just predict!) **Record** your prediction.

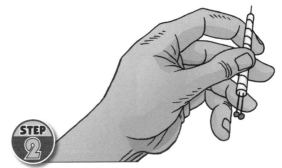

STEP 2

Carefully **stick** two pins in the bottom of the candle. (They should stick straight down, but don't have to be pushed in very far.) **Predict** what would happen to the candle and pins if you dropped them in the bottle. **Record** your prediction.

STEP 3

Gently **place** the candle in the water, pins down, wick up. Keep the wick dry! The candle should float upright with the wick just out of the water. (**Add** or **remove** pins if needed.) Now **predict** what might happen to the candle when it burns.

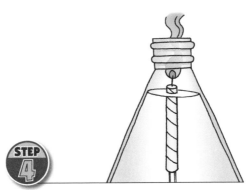

STEP 4

Watch as the teacher lights your candle. **Observe** as it burns. (Pay close attention to the distance between the wick and the water.) **Record** the results. **Share** and **compare** observations with your research team.

WHAT HAPPENED?

As you know, all **matter** on Earth is constantly being **pulled** downward by **gravity**. To keep an object from sinking in the water, gravity has to be overcome (**pushed**) by another **force**. The opposing force we see pushing in this activity is called **buoyancy**.

When you float on an air mattress in a swimming pool, you experience buoyancy. The air mattress is so buoyant that it not only can float its own **weight**, but float your weight as well!

So why didn't the candle burn "down"? As it burned, it lost weight. (Remember, weight is a measurement of the pull of gravity.) Since it weighed less, it was pulled down less, so it became more **buoyant**. In fact, if you let it continue to burn, there would be very little candle left before the water finally reached the flame!

WHAT WE LEARNED

1 **What did you predict in Step 1?**
How did your prediction reflect what actually happened?

_____

_____

_____

_____

_____

_____

_____

2 **What did you predict in Step 2?**
How did your prediction reflect what actually happened?

_____

_____

_____

_____

_____

_____

_____

3 What did you predict in Step 3?
How did your prediction reflect what actually happened?

_____

_____

_____

_____

_____

_____

4 Describe what happened to the candle's buoyancy
as it burned and why this occurred.

_____

_____

_____

_____

_____

_____

5 What do you think would have happened in a much
larger container using a much larger candle? Why?

_____

_____

_____

_____

_____

_____

CONCLUSION

Gravity is always pulling everything down. Buoyancy is the difference between the downward pull of gravity and the push of the liquid the object is floating in.

FOOD FOR THOUGHT

Matthew 5:14-16 The candle you used in this activity was a great example. As it burned, it didn't just sink away. Instead it kept rising higher, letting its light show!

In this Scripture, Jesus told his followers to do something similar. He asked us to let the love of God that's inside us show through. We can show God's love in the things that we do and the way we live our lives.

Do you want to hide your light — or be a city on the hill, with the light of Jesus shining bright for all to see?

JOURNAL My Science Notes

FLAME OUT

LESSON 17

FOCUS Force Transfer

OBJECTIVE To explore how forces can be moved

OVERVIEW Our modern world depends on moving forces from one place to another. We'll explore that idea in this activity, by using a simple device to put out a candle flame without touching it.

WHAT TO DO

STEP 1

Watch as the teacher lights your candle. **Place** one team member about a foot from the flame. **Ask** him/her to blow the candle out. (The teacher will relight it.) Now **discuss** ways you might put out the candle using only an empty oatmeal container.

STEP 2

Remove the lid of the oatmeal container. Reach inside and **push** the bottom a little so it's slightly domed outward. From about one foot away, **point** the open end of the container at the candle and **whack** it on the bottom one time. **Record** the results.

STEP 3

Carefully **cut** a half inch hole in the center of the lid. Reach inside the container and **push** the bottom out again as before. **Replace** the lid, making sure the bottom doesn't pop back in. **Predict** how you might use this modified device to put out the flame.

STEP 4

Aim the hole at the candle flame. **Whack** the container on the bottom. (If nothing happens, push the bottom back out and try again.) **Record** the results. Now carefully **review** each step in this activity. **Share** and **compare** observations with your research team.

FORCES **77**

WHAT HAPPENED?

Much of our modern world is based on **transferring** forces from one place to another. In Step 1, you transferred a **force** (the moving air) from your mouth to the candle, performing **work** (moving the air across a distance to put out the flame).

In Step 4, you used the oatmeal container as a **mechanical substitute** for the muscles of your mouth. The whack you gave the container was transferred to the candle, **extinguishing** the flame.

Transferring forces across long distances is a vital part of the complicated world of technology we live in. Examples include **transmitting** electricity through wires, **broadcasting** radio or television programs, or **beaming** light through fiber optic cables to a computer.

WHAT WE LEARNED

1 **Describe the transfer of forces that took place in Step 1.**

_____

_____

_____

_____

_____

_____

2 **What were some ideas your team had in Step 1 for putting out the flame using the container? Which ones might have worked? Why?**

_____

_____

_____

_____

_____

_____

3 What did you predict in Step 3?
How did your prediction reflect what actually happened in Step 4?

_____

_____

_____

_____

_____

_____

4 Compare Step 2 with Step 4. How were the results different?
What role did the hole in the lid play in Step 4?

_____

_____

_____

_____

_____

_____

5 Give at least two other examples of transferring forces
from one place to another.

_____

_____

_____

_____

_____

_____

_____

CONCLUSION

Forces can be transferred from one place to another — sometimes over very long distances. Force can also be focused into a more concentrated form in order to be more useful and efficient. Modern life depends on the transfer of forces.

FOOD FOR THOUGHT

Proverbs 13:9 In this activity, you transferred a force from the bottom of the container to the candle — and the flame went out!

Scripture also talks about a moving force, God's power! When our hearts are sad and empty, God's touch can fill them with power, joy, and love.

Proverbs talks about how the power of God's love results in our lives being full of light. But without God's power, our lives can be dark and gloomy. Stay close to God and let his power and love shine through you!

JOURNAL My Science Notes

_____

_____

_____

_____

_____

_____

_____

_____

_____

_____

_____

_____

_____

_____

_____

_____

_____

_____

NAME _____

FOCUS Flight

OBJECTIVE To explore how forces allow flight

OVERVIEW You've discovered that nothing moves without forces. But how do forces help things fly? This activity provides an answer with a "twist!"

WHAT TO DO

STEP 1

Remove the "Twisty T" page from the back of your work-text (page 171). **Cut out** the Twisty T flyer using the solid blue lines. (Do not cut any red lines. Red lines are for folding only!)

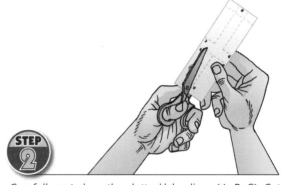

STEP 2

Carefully **cut** along the dotted blue lines (A, B, C). Cut only as far as the lines go! Now **fold** along line D one way, and along line E the other. If you look at your Twisty T from the side, it should now look like the letter T.

STEP 3

Fold in the sides at lines F and G so your Twisty T has a smaller shaft. Now **fold** the bottom up at line H to make a tab at the bottom. (Make sure the wings are tipped up slightly.) Now **examine** your Twisty T and make notes about what you see.

STEP 4

Here comes the fun part! **Toss** your Twisty T into the air. It should wobble skyward, stop, and begin spinning to the ground in a graceful spiral. Now carefully **review** each step in this activity. **Share** and **compare** observations with your research team.

FORCES **81**

WHAT HAPPENED?

Forces always come in **pairs**. Every force has an **opposing force**. For instance, when you stand up, the force of your muscles fights against the force of **gravity**.

In this activity, gravity was trying to **pull** your Twisty T flyer down. But your Twisty T flyer resisted gravity by spinning like a top and slowing its fall. This showed us that there was another force in action, too. So what happened?

As it fell, your Twisty T flyer's wing flaps were given a slight **twist**. The twist turned those strips of paper into wings, creating **lift** (a backwards **push** against gravity). Lift is a force that's caused when air rushes over the top of a surface faster than it does the bottom. It's the force that allows for flight. Although gravity will eventually triumph, the force of lift allows us to slow the descent of the Twisty T.

WHAT WE LEARNED

1 Describe the Twisty T flyer after you cut it out in Step 1. Would it fly like this? Why or why not?

_____

_____

_____

_____

_____

_____

_____

2 Compare the Twisty T flyer at the end of Step 3 with what it looked like at the end of Step 1. How was it similar? How was it different?

_____

_____

_____

_____

_____

_____

3 What were the two forces demonstrated in this activity? How did they interact with each other?

_____

_____

_____

_____

_____

_____

4 What kind of aircraft does the Twisty T flyer remind you of? How are they similar? How are they different?

_____

_____

_____

_____

_____

_____

5 Compare the flight of your Twisty T flyer with the flyers made by other teams. List some factors that might make them fly differently.

_____

_____

_____

_____

_____

_____

CONCLUSION

Nothing moves without the influence of a force. Forces come in pairs, and every force has an opposing force. Under controlled circumstances, the force of lift can allow an object to fly.

FOOD FOR THOUGHT

James 4:7 Your Twisty T flyer did a great job resisting the pull of gravity. But eventually, gravity won, and the flyer ended up on the ground. Even a powerful helicopter can't resist gravity forever. Sooner or later, it has to come down.

Scripture tells us that we must "resist" the devil. Yet Satan is powerful, and if we only rely on our own strength, eventually he'll drag us down. But the first part of this verse offers us an "opposing force." James tells us to submit (or give) ourselves to God. If we do this, then God's power will overcome the force of the devil, and we will be kept safe from harm!

JOURNAL My Science Notes

Earth Science

Earth Science is the study of **earth** and **sky**. In this section, you'll explore the structure of our planet (rocks, crystals, volcanos), the atmosphere (air, clouds), and related systems (water cycles, air pressure, weather). Grades 7 and 8 reach out even further with a look at the solar system and stars.

NAME _____

VACUUM PUMP

FOCUS Air Pressure

OBJECTIVE To explore air pressure as a force

OVERVIEW We're surrounded by an ocean of air. So why doesn't this huge mass of air crush us? In this activity, we'll find out more about how air pressure works.

WHAT TO DO

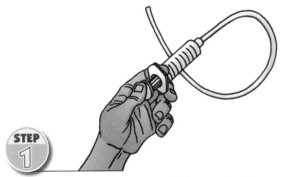

STEP 1

Push the handle of the syringe all the way in. Now **attach** one end of the aquarium hose to the end of the syringe. **Pull** the syringe handle out, then **push** it back in. **Watch** for any observable changes in the syringe or hose. **Record** your observations.

STEP 2

Push the one-hole stopper firmly into the neck of the empty bottle. **Push** the free end of the hose through the stopper's hole. Use clay to completely **seal** the hole around the hose. **Predict** why it's important to make sure the hose is well sealed.

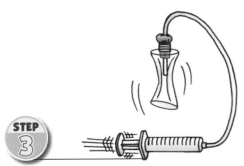

STEP 3

Gently **pull** the syringe handle back and **watch** the bottle's sides very closely. **Describe** what you see. (If nothing happens, check the seal. You may need to gently touch the sides of the bottle to encourage movement.)

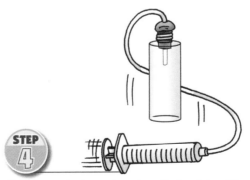

STEP 4

Slowly **push** the syringe handle back in. **Observe** what happens. Now **review** each step in this activity. **Share** and **compare** observations with your research team.

What causes **air pressure**? Think of billions of little air **molecules** constantly pushing against each other, and against everything around them (including you!).

If an open bottle is setting on your work surface, the air molecules are pushing with the same amount of force both inside and outside the bottle. Since the force of the air (air pressure) is equal, nothing happens.

But when you **pulled** on the syringe handle, you pulled some air molecules out of the sealed bottle. Suddenly, there were more molecules outside than inside. The bottle couldn't stand the difference, so it collapsed. When you **pushed** on the handle, you forced air molecules back into the bottle. This replaced enough of them to push back evenly against the surrounding air so that the bottle returned to its original shape!

1 Describe what happened in Step 1. What effect was produced by pushing and pulling on the syringe handle?

_____

_____

_____

_____

_____

_____

2 In Step 2, why was the seal around the aquarium hose important? What did a good seal allow you to control?

_____

_____

_____

_____

_____

_____

3 Compare Steps 3 and 4. What happened to the bottle when you pulled the handle? What happened when you pushed?

_____

_____

_____

_____

_____

_____

4 Based on what you've learned, explain why the huge "ocean of air" that surrounds us doesn't crush us.

_____

_____

_____

_____

_____

_____

5 If we sealed the bottle at normal air pressure, then put it into a space where the air pressure was much higher, what would happen?

_____

_____

_____

_____

_____

_____

CONCLUSION

Air pressure is the force of the air pressing on everything around us. Changes in air pressure can result in changes to physical objects.

FOOD FOR THOUGHT

Romans 16:20 Sometimes life just isn't fair. Problems pile up until you feel like the whole world is crushing in on you!

While the bottle couldn't withstand the crushing pressure of the air, God can help you withstand the crushing pressure of the world! He is the great equalizer. His power is always there for you, providing the support you need when the weight of the world presses in. All you have to do is ask.

Remember, the bottle didn't have a choice — but you do!

JOURNAL   My Science Notes

AIR GLUE

LESSON 20

FOCUS Air Pressure

OBJECTIVE To explore effects of air pressure

OVERVIEW Air pressure can be a very strong push or pull force. Sometimes it even acts like a kind of glue! In this activity, we'll find out how that can happen.

WHAT TO DO

STEP 1

Fold a piece of newspaper into a square about six inches across. **Place** the newspaper in the middle of the tray and **soak** it thoroughly. **Set** a wide-mouth jar upside down on the paper. **Lift** the jar and **observe** what happens.

STEP 2

Remove the jar. **Cut** a single sheet of dry newspaper into a square about ten inches across. **Crumple** the newspaper slightly and **push** it completely inside the jar. **Place** the wide-mouth jar back on the wet newspaper as before. Now **lift** the jar and **observe** what happens.

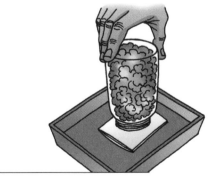

STEP 3

Set the jar back on the table with the open end facing up. **Observe** as your teacher sets fire to the newspaper in the jar, and then turns the jar upside down on the wet newspaper. **Observe** what is happening inside the jar.

STEP 4

Watch the fire go out, then **wait** until the jar is cool enough to touch. (Note: The jar can be hot even if it doesn't look like it!) Slowly **lift** the jar and **observe** what happens. **Review** each step in this activity. **Share** and **compare** observations with other research teams.

WHAT HAPPENED?

The **heat energy** from the fire made the **air molecules** move faster and faster, pushing them further apart. As the fire grew, a lot of air molecules **pushed** their way out through the mouth of the jar, resulting in fewer air molecules inside.

When your teacher flipped the jar upside down, the fire (and fewer air molecules) were trapped. As the fire went out, the molecules left inside the jar started slowing down, and the air pressure fell. Since the jar was sealed by wet paper, no air could get back in to help **equalize** (balance) the pressure. Since there were fewer air molecules in the jar, the pressure **inside** became much lower than pressure **outside** the jar.

When you lifted the jar, it stuck tightly to the tray. The force holding it was the higher outside air pressure. The air was pushing on the jar, trying to get back inside!

WHAT WE LEARNED

1 In Step 1, why didn't the jar stick to the tray?

2 Compare Step 1 with Step 2. What was similar?
What was different? What happened when you lifted the jar?

3 In Step 3, what happened inside the jar? What effect did this have on the air molecules in the jar?

4 Compare Step 4 with Step 2. How were they similar? How were they different? What happened when you lifted the jar?

5 Based on what you've learned, why is tossing an aerosol can into a fire **not** a safe thing to do? What might happen to it?

CONCLUSION

Air pressure can be a powerful force, either pushing or pulling. Changes in air pressure can be caused by many things. Air molecules are constantly trying to equalize pressure in and around objects.

FOOD FOR THOUGHT

Mark 12:30   In Lesson 1, we talked about the pressure that problems can place on our lives. But sometimes pressures come from the people around us, not events or things. Even our closest friends can sometimes cause us pain.

But remember, God can equalize any pressure if we only call on him!

This Scripture shows us how it's done. It reminds us not to focus on pushing our problems away, but on pushing to get closer to God! When God is by our side, living in our hearts, we can handle any kind of pressure.

JOURNAL My Science Notes

NAME _____

BAROMETER BOTTLE

FOCUS Barometers

OBJECTIVE To explore how air pressure is measured

OVERVIEW In Lessons 1 and 2, we learned that air pressure is a force and that it affects people and materials. To learn more about air pressure, let's build a simple device to measure it.

WHAT TO DO

STEP 1

Hold the balloon with the neck toward you. **Slip** one side of a pair of scissors inside the balloon, then **cut** down the balloon to the tip. **Unfold** the balloon so it looks like a sheet of rubber.

STEP 2

Gently **stretch** the balloon over the mouth of the jar. Make sure it's even and flat. Now **wrap** a rubber band around the top of the jar to hold the balloon tightly in place. (Have a team member help if needed.) **Trim** any rough edges.

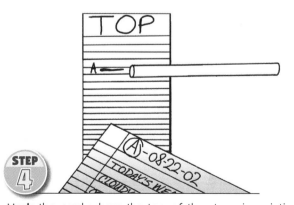

STEP 3

Carefully **tape** one end of the small white straw to the center of the balloon. **Write** "top" on one end of an index card, then **stand** the card so it's almost touching the straw. **Move** so you're eye level with the top of the bottle, then **sight** along the straw toward the index card.

STEP 4

Mark the card where the top of the straw is pointing. **Label** the mark "A." In your journal **print** "A," followed by the date. **Add** comments about the current weather. **Repeat** this step each day. At the end of the week, **share** and **compare** observations with your research team.

Pressure is a term that describes how much something is **pushing** on a given area. Since air is constantly pushing on us, why don't we feel smashed? It's because our bodies push back with just as much force as the air.

The **weather** in your area is different every day. As the weather changes, there's a different amount of air pushing down. Scientists and meteorologists measure this change in air pressure (also called **barometric pressure**) using barometers.

Although **barometers** come in many different shapes and sizes, most are based on a sealed container of air. The simple barometer you made reflects air pressure changes because as the outside pressure increases or decreases, the air trapped in the jar expands or contracts, making the balloon swell up or sag down.

WHAT WE LEARNED

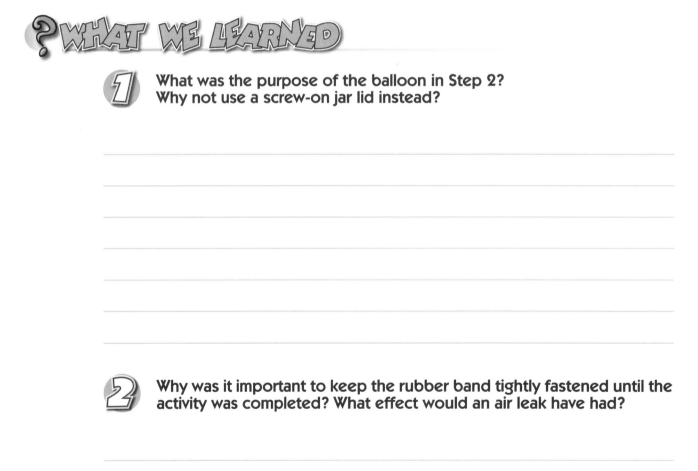

1 What was the purpose of the balloon in Step 2? Why not use a screw-on jar lid instead?

2 Why was it important to keep the rubber band tightly fastened until the activity was completed? What effect would an air leak have had?

3 What caused the air in the jar to expand or contract?
How did you know the air inside was expanding or contracting?

4 In step 4, what sort of comments did you add after recording the level of the straw each day? How might such a record be helpful?

5 Based on what you've learned, what would the straw do if an approaching storm caused the barometric pressure to fall? Why?

CONCLUSION

Air pressure is always around us. Weather can cause changes in air pressure. Scientists and meteorologists use barometers to measure these pressure changes.

FOOD FOR THOUGHT

Luke 8:22-24 The weather often determines what we wear, what we do, and sometimes even where we go. A barometer is a good tool to help us forecast the weather. But no matter how carefully we keep track of it, we can't **change** the weather even a tiny bit!

Scripture tells us that the disciples were amazed (and even a little frightened) to see Jesus calmly quiet an angry storm. Sometimes we forget the awesome power of our God. If God is powerful enough to control the weather, isn't he powerful enough to do what's best for those who learn to trust him?

 **My Science Notes**

NAME _____

FOCUS Water Cycle

OBJECTIVE To explore physical changes in water

OVERVIEW There's a lot of moisture on this planet. You can often find it even in places that seem completely dry. This activity is based on a desert survival trick that can produce a little water seemingly from nowhere!

WHAT TO DO

STEP 1

With your research team, **dig** a hole about eighteen inches across and a foot deep. (**Pile** the dirt neatly so you can refill the hole after this activity.) **Remove** all the loose dirt, plus any creatures you find. Once the hole is empty and fairly smooth, **examine** it closely for any signs of water. **Record** what you see.

STEP 2

Carefully **place** your can in the center of the hole. Be sure it is as level as you can make it. **Examine** the can closely to make sure it is clean and dry. **Record** what you see.

STEP 3

Cover the hole with the plastic, making sure it's smooth and flat. **Place** a marble-size rock in the middle of the plastic (directly over the can), letting the plastic sag about 2 inches. Now **pile** dirt around the edges to anchor the plastic firmly! **Examine** the plastic for any signs of water. **Record** what you see.

STEP 4

Check the plastic each day to make sure it's firmly anchored and not touching the can. At the end of the week, **remove** the rock and the dirt, then carefully **examine** the plastic and can for signs of moisture. **Share** and **compare** observations with your research team.

WHAT HAPPENED?

So where did the water come from and how did it get in the can? First, the plastic made the hole into a tiny greenhouse. This let the sun's **heat** (energy) change any moisture in the soil into a **gas** (water vapor) through a process called **evaporation**.

As the moisture tried to evaporate, the plastic sheet trapped it inside. As long as the sun was shining, the **moisture** (water vapor) just kept floating around the hole. When the sun went down and the air cooled, the plastic became colder than the air in the hole. When the water vapor hit the cool plastic, it lost a lot of its heat and turned back into a **liquid** (water) through a process called **condensation**.

Finally, **gravity** pulled the water droplets down the angled sides of the plastic sheet where they collected at the bottom, then eventually dropped into the can!

WHAT WE LEARNED

1 Describe Step 1. What did the hole look like when you completed this step? Did you find any water?

_____

_____

_____

_____

_____

_____

2 Describe Step 2. Was there any water in the can when you completed this step?

_____

_____

_____

_____

_____

_____

3 Describe Step 3. Was there any water on the plastic when you completed this step?

4 If there was no sign of water in Steps 1, 2, and 3, then where did the water in the can come from?

5 Describe the process of evaporation. Describe condensation. How are these processes important to our weather?

! CONCLUSION

Water on Earth comes in three different forms — gas, liquid, and solid. Various forces can cause water to change from one form (or "state") into another.

FOOD FOR THOUGHT

John 4:10-15 All living things need water to survive. Without regular supplies of water, our bodies would quickly shrivel up and die.

In this Scripture, Jesus talks about another kind of water — water for the soul. In the same way we need water to keep our physical bodies alive, we also need "living water" from God to keep our souls alive.

By staying close to Jesus and learning to trust in the Father, we can have an unending supply.

JOURNAL **My Science Notes**

NAME _____

SEDIMENTARY SANDWICH

FOCUS Geology

OBJECTIVE To explore sedimentary rock

OVERVIEW God created an interesting planet for us to explore! For example, there are many kinds of rocks! One kind of rock is made from layers of sediments (like sand or mud). In this activity, we'll discover how sedimentary rock is formed.

WHAT TO DO

STEP 1

Review the rules for this activity with your research team:
Rule A: **Clean** your hands, your work surface, and any utensils before beginning.
Rule B: **Cover** every layer of your sandwich completely with the layer above and below it.
Rule C: Carefully **clean** your work area and **dispose** of any debris following Step 4.

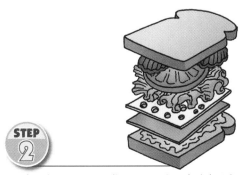

STEP 2

To begin your "Sedimentary Sandwich," **lay** a slice of bread on a paper towel. Now **choose** and **add** sandwich ingredients one layer at a time. (Use any order you wish, but don't forget Rule B!) **Observe** any differences in your team members' choice of ingredients or the order they apply ingredients.

STEP 3

When you're finished, **raise** your hand so the teacher knows you're ready for Step 3. When it's your turn, **watch** closely as the teacher cuts your sandwich exactly in half.

STEP 4

Separate the two halves and closely **observe** the cut edges. You may slightly separate layers for a better view. Make notes and drawings about what you see, then **share** and **compare** observations with your research team.

As you discovered, layers of ingredients can be stacked together to make a tasty sandwich. Layers of ingredients can also be stacked together to make a kind of **rock**. (Of course, the ingredients in the rock aren't nearly as tasty!)

The layers of **sedimentary rock** are composed of **sediments** — materials carried by wind or moving water. Sediments can be as large as pebbles or fine as dust. As wind or water slows down, sediments drop and **gravity** settles them into layers. As time passes, these layers are covered up by other **deposits** (new layers of sediment).

Over time, the increasing **weight** of the materials begins to squeeze these layers of mud, sand, silt, and dust together. Eventually they are **compressed** into solid rock.

WHAT WE LEARNED

1 **Why do you think it was so important in Step 1 to clean the area and equipment carefully before beginning the activity?**

_____

_____

_____

_____

_____

_____

_____

2 **Sedimentary rock is made of layers laid down over time. Which layer of your sandwich represents the oldest layer? The youngest? Why?**

_____

_____

_____

_____

_____

_____

3 In Step 3, your teacher's knife made a "cross-section" of the sandwich. What natural processes might do something similar to the ground?

4 Look at the question above. What man-made or mechanical processes might create cross-sections in the ground?

5 Your sandwich looked different from other sandwiches. Why? Roads cut through hills leave different-looking cross-sections. Why?

CONCLUSION

One type of sedimentary rock is made when layers of sediment build up and are squeezed by their own weight until they eventually turn into solid rock.

FOOD FOR THOUGHT

1 Corinthians 12:4-11 Even though similar ingredients were used, every sandwich was different from all the others. It's much the same with human beings.

This Scripture reminds us that God has given each of us special and distinct gifts to be used in his service. Perhaps you have musical talent. You may have art ability or athletic skills. Maybe you have the ability to teach. All of us have gifts from God that are molded and formed into us.

Remember, God made you as a unique creation!

JOURNAL My Science Notes

MINI CORE SAMPLE

LESSON 24

FOCUS Earth's Structure

OBJECTIVE To explore core sampling

OVERVIEW The earth is made of many different materials, but we can usually only see the top layer. In this activity, we'll explore one method scientists use to study what's below the surface!

WHAT TO DO

STEP 1

Pour about an inch of sand, an inch of potting soil, and an inch of aquarium gravel into a wide-mouth jar. (Do not completely fill the jar!) **Put** the lid on the jar and **shake** the mixture thoroughly. **Look** through the sides of the jar at the results. **Record** what you observe.

STEP 2

Remove the lid from the jar and slowly **add** water until the mixture is saturated. Keep adding water until it's an inch over the mixture. **Put** the lid back on the jar again and **shake** it thoroughly. (Be sure the lid is tight!) **Set** the jar in a safe location until tomorrow.

STEP 3

[next day] **Look** through the sides of the jar at the layers and **record** what you see. Now slowly **push** a large straw straight down into the material. **Push** it to the bottom. **Put** your thumb over the opening, and **pull** it out slowly. Gently **lay** the straw on its side on a paper towel. Let it dry for two days.

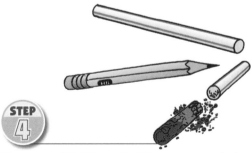

STEP 4

[two days later] Now that the core sample is dry, use a pencil eraser to gently **push** the sample out of the straw. Don't force it! (Your teacher will help if needed.) **Examine** your sample. Now **review** each step in this activity. **Share** and **compare** observations with your research team.

WHAT HAPPENED?

Over long periods of time, **sediments** build up in deep layers on the bottom of streams, rivers, lakes, and oceans. Scientists drill through the **sedimentary rock** and remove long plugs of the materials they have drilled through.

These cylinders are called **core samples**. Geologists sometimes use core samples to locate useful substances like oil and natural gas. Biologists use core samples to study the floor of the ocean, polar icecaps, and even endangered wetlands.

Core samples can also serve as a kind of "time capsule." Minerals and other ancient substances (including fossils) in core samples provide scientists with clues about the environment of long ago. By analyzing these materials, they can catch a glimpse of what was happening in the years when the sediments were first laid down.

WHAT WE LEARNED

1 Compare the ingredients in Step 1 with common materials found on the Earth's surface. How are they similar? How are they different?

2 What does the shaking represent in step 2? What happened to the biggest pieces? What happened to the smallest pieces?

3 Why was it important to put your thumb over the end of the straw in Step 3? What might have happened if you didn't?

_____

_____

_____

_____

_____

_____

4 Compare the core sample from Step 4 with the materials in the jar. How is it similar? How is it different?

_____

_____

_____

_____

_____

_____

5 Based on what you've learned, what kinds of places might yield interesting core samples? Why?

_____

_____

_____

_____

_____

_____

CONCLUSION

Although scientists can't actually see what's under the Earth's surface, core sampling provides a clue. Core samples allow researchers to gather specific information about layers of material far below ground.

FOOD FOR THOUGHT

Job 38:4-7 Scientists are constantly probing and sampling the earth. There are so many amazing things to discover about the structure of this wonderful world that God created! The deeper scientists dig into the Earth, the more they learn.

It's the same with God's Word. The deeper we dig into it, the more we learn. Just as science helps us understand our world, the Scriptures help us understand the God who made the world! There are so many exciting things to learn!

Dig deep and discover more about the awesome God we serve!

JOURNAL My Science Notes

NAME _____

TUBULAR VOLCANO

FOCUS Volcanoes

OBJECTIVE To explore the action of volcanoes

OVERVIEW Volcanoes are so powerful, they literally move mountains! In this activity, we'll build a model of a volcano so you can explore these explosive forces — but without endangering yourself or your classroom!

WHAT TO DO

STEP 1

Push the stopper firmly into one end of the hose. **Hold** the hose upright (stopper at the bottom) and **pour** in a tablespoon of sodium bicarbonate (baking soda). **Tap** the hose to make sure the soda reaches the bottom. **Examine** the hose and **record** your observations.

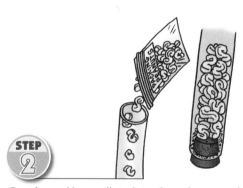

STEP 2

Break packing pellets into tiny pieces and **drop** them down the tube. (Tap the tube to make sure they reach the bottom.) These pieces represent solid materials like rocks or soil affected by the action of a volcano. Now **examine** the "loaded" tube and **record** your observations.

STEP 3

Fill the paper cup about one-third full of acetic acid (vinegar). **Add** a small squirt of dishwashing soap. Gently **swirl** the cup to mix these ingredients together. **Examine** the mixture and **record** your observations.

STEP 4

Hold the tube upright (stopper at bottom) and carefully **pour** the liquid into the tube. **Watch** it flow past the packing pellets and react with the dry material at the bottom. **Record** what you see. **Share** and **compare** observations with your research team.

WHAT HAPPENED?

In May of 1980, Mount St. Helens exploded in a violent **eruption**. The entire top blew off, leaving a crater nearly two miles square! Blast winds of over 300 miles per hour flattened entire forests! The explosion destroyed 27 bridges, nearly 200 homes, and over 185 miles of highways! **Ash** covered everything for hundreds of square miles.

This shows the tremendous **force** of a **volcano**. Its **energy** comes from **gas** trapped in the **lava**. When the conditions are right, it's a lot like a bottle of soda pop that's been shaken violently. It looks pretty safe until the lid comes off — then KABOOM!

Your Tubular Volcano was a good imitation of a volcano, but a whole lot safer! The **chemical reaction** of the vinegar and baking soda provided the gas for your "explosion."

WHAT WE LEARNED

1 **Describe Step 1. What ingredients did you add to the tube? Did you see any signs of gas bubbles?**

_____

_____

_____

_____

_____

_____

2 **Describe Step 2. What additional ingredients were added to the tube? Did you see any signs of gas bubbles?**

_____

_____

_____

_____

_____

3 Describe Step 3. What ingredients did you mix together in the cup? Did you see any signs of gas bubbles?

_____

_____

_____

_____

_____

_____

4 Describe Step 4. What ingredients did you add to the tube? Did you see any gas bubbles? What happened to the packing pellets?

_____

_____

_____

_____

_____

_____

_____

5 What force provided the reaction in this activity? What force drives the powerful explosive and destructive behavior of some volcanoes?

_____

_____

_____

_____

_____

_____

_____

CONCLUSION

Volcanoes can change the Earth's surface drastically! Many volcanic eruptions are driven by the sudden release of enormous pressure from gases as rock is moved or broken inside the earth.

FOOD FOR THOUGHT

Isaiah 54:10 Volcanoes and earthquakes are violent examples of the powerful forces that are sometimes found in nature.

This Scripture reminds us that no matter how violent the world becomes, God will always be there for us! We may choose to walk away from God, but God never walks away from us. He never breaks his promises.

If we choose to be God's children, then nothing, not even the most powerful volcano, can separate us from his love.

 **My Science Notes**

PHONY FOSSIL

FOCUS Fossils

OBJECTIVE To explore fossilization

OVERVIEW Fossils give us clues about the kinds of plants and animals that lived in the distant past. In this activity, we'll learn about a common kind of fossil.

WHAT TO DO

STEP 1

Work with your research team on this activity. First, **mix** 1 cup of flour, 1 cup of new coffee grounds, 1/2 cup cold coffee, and 1/2 cup salt in a bowl. **Stir** thoroughly. This mixture will become the "instant rock" you'll use to create your fossil imprint.

STEP 2

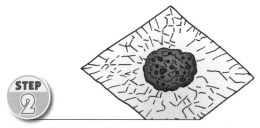

Dump the entire mixture on a large piece of waxed paper. **Flatten** it until it's an even thickness — about 3/4 of an inch works best. **Examine** your instant rock and **record** what you see.

STEP 3

Pick up your "fossil" (dog biscuit). Now carefully **press** it into the instant rock. **Wiggle** it gently to make a good impression. Don't press too hard or your rock will break! **Remove** the fossil and **dry** the rock overnight.

STEP 4

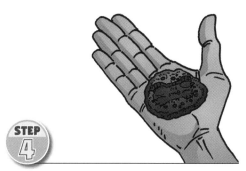

[next day] Now that it's had a chance to harden, **examine** your phony fossil! (Handle it carefully because instant rock is much more brittle than the real thing.) **Review** each step in this activity. **Share** and **compare** observations with your research team.

WHAT HAPPENED?

Any physical evidence left behind by a dead **organism** is called a **fossil**. A fossil could be a physical part of the creature, like a bone or a tooth. But a preserved animal track or impression can also be a fossil. Almost any material that shows us something about the organism when it was alive can be called a fossil.

The fossil that you just modeled is called an **imprint** or a **mold** fossil. This kind of fossil must be formed in very soft materials, such as sand or silt. The ancient animal or plant that made the shape is completely gone, but its shape is left behind!

Another type of fossil is the **cast** fossil. This fossil is made when fine materials like clay or mud fill an older molded fossil, and then these materials harden. Since the cast fossil gets its shape from the mold, it usually looks very much like the original creature.

WHAT WE LEARNED

1 **What were the characteristics of the mix in Step 1?**
Why did this make it a good material for making impressions?

_____

_____

_____

_____

_____

_____

2 **What was the purpose of the wax paper in Step 2?**
Why was getting the mix an equal thickness important?

_____

_____

_____

_____

_____

_____

3 What parts of a living creature are most likely to be found as fossils? Why? What parts are not likely to be fossils? Why?

_____

_____

_____

_____

_____

_____

_____

4 What is the difference between an imprint fossil and a cast fossil? How are they similar? How are they different?

_____

_____

_____

_____

_____

_____

_____

5 Based on what you've learned, why can't scientists tell exactly how a creature looked by studying its fossils?

_____

_____

_____

_____

_____

_____

_____

! CONCLUSION

For a fossil to be preserved, conditions must be perfect. Fossils are formed in several different ways. Fossils provide us with information about how organisms looked and behaved when they were alive.

FOOD FOR THOUGHT

Genesis 1:26-27 When we look at a fossil, we often see only a portion of an image of a creature. Without more information, there's really no way to tell exactly what that creature looked like. With only fossil evidence available, we have to come up with the best picture we can, based on what we know.

Scripture tells us that man was made in the image of God. When people look at us, how much of a glimpse of God do they see? Do they see God's kindness and compassion? Do they see God's willing service? Do they see God's watchful care? Remember, the closer we get to God, the more accurately we can reflect his image!

JOURNAL My Science Notes

NAME _____

FOCUS Crystallization

OBJECTIVE To explore how groundwater forms cave formations

OVERVIEW Although a drop of water looks clear, it can carry many minerals inside. Water dripping from cave ceilings sometimes creates stalactites – those rock "icicles" you see hanging in caves. This activity will help you understand how stalactites are formed.

WHAT TO DO

STEP 1

Fill a paper cup 1/2 full of warm water. Slowly **add** three level capfuls of magnesium sulfate. **Stir** constantly with the craft stick, dissolving as many crystals as you can. Follow the same process with a second cup. **Observe** the two cups and **record** what you see.

STEP 2

Cut a piece of string 16" long. **Tie** a washer tightly to each end of the string. **Move** the cups to the location your teacher shows you, then carefully **drop** the washers and string into one of the cups and **soak** them overnight.

STEP 3

[next day] **Place** the cups side by side. **Lift** one washer from where it's soaking and **place** it carefully in the other cup. **Separate** the cups and **place** a piece of paper between them. Slowly **move** them closer until the string is about an inch from the paper. **Draw** what you see.

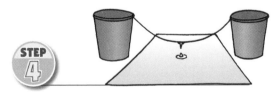

STEP 4

Let the string/cups set for the rest of the week. Do not disturb them in any way! At the end of the week, **look** carefully at the lowest part of the string. **Record** and **draw** what you see. **Share** and **compare** observations with your research team.

WHAT HAPPENED?

When it rains, water soaks into the ground. Where does this **groundwater** go from there? In some parts of the country, it flows into caves. The water dripping through the ceiling is full of **dissolved minerals** that the groundwater picked up while soaking through the ground. Sometimes the water **evaporates** while still on the ceiling, leaving behind the minerals it was carrying. This forms **stalactites**. Sometimes water drops to the cave's floor, leaving the minerals there. This forms **stalagmites**.

The "drip, evaporate, leave minerals behind" process that forms stalactites and stalagmites is similar to what happened to the string in this activity. The magnesium sulfate **solution** dripped down to the lowest point on the string due to **gravity**. As the water evaporated, the solution changed back to its **solid** state, forming crystals. This process is also known as **crystallization**.

WHAT WE LEARNED

1 **What happened to the pieces of magnesium sulfate you poured in the warm water during Step 1? What's another name for a "mixed" liquid?**

_____

_____

_____

_____

_____

_____

2 **Describe Step 2. Why was it important to soak the string overnight?**

_____

_____

_____

_____

_____

_____

3 Describe Step 3. Why was it important to let the string sag between the cups?

_____

_____

_____

_____

_____

_____

4 What appeared on the string in step 4?
Where did this material come from?

_____

_____

_____

_____

_____

_____

5 Explain how this activity reflects what happens in caves.

_____

_____

_____

_____

_____

_____

CONCLUSION

Water that seeps and flows underground is called groundwater. As water moves through soil and rock, it dissolves various minerals and carries them along with it. When the water evaporates, the minerals are left behind.

FOOD FOR THOUGHT

1 Peter 3:4 For your crystals to grow properly, they need a calm, quiet place. Too much moving air, a little vibration, or someone moving the containers around can really mess things up!

This Scripture reminds us our spirits are made for calm and quiet, too. But Satan doesn't want us to spend quiet time with God, so he does everything he can to create disturbances in our lives! His world is noisy, pushy, loud, and rude. And without a time of quiet and peace, it's hard for God's love to grow in our hearts.

Be sure to spend some quiet time in prayer every day.

 **My Science Notes**

Energy & MATTER

LESSONS 28-36

Energy and Matter

In this section, you'll learn about the different states and unique properties of matter. You'll discover new things about light and sound. You'll explore physical and chemical reactions. Some grades will explore related concepts like circuits, currents, and convection.

PAPER WAVES

FOCUS Wave structure

OBJECTIVE To explore the parts and functions of waves

OVERVIEW There are many kinds of waves. Some examples are ocean waves, sound waves, and light waves. Waves help us see, hear, and feel things. In this activity, you'll find out more about how waves work.

WHAT TO DO

STEP 1

Pick up the Paper Wave pad and **hold** it in one hand. Gently **lift** the top sheet about 6 inches. (Do not pull it loose from the pad!) **Examine** the pad closely and **record** what you observe.

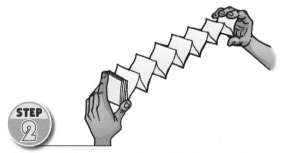

STEP 2

Continue lifting the top sheet. Slowly **pass** it to a team member. **Hold** on to the bottom sheet and carefully **stretch** the linked papers out. Now **turn** them so the "waves" go up and down. (Don't pull too tight or it will break!) **Sketch** what this "paper wave" looks like.

STEP 3

Now **stretch** your wave out near a strong light like a bright window or a lamp. **Observe** the shadow the wave makes. Slowly **move** one end of the wave up and down. (Gently please!) **Observe** what happens and **record** what you observe.

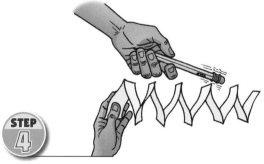

STEP 4

With your partner, continue holding your stretched wave. **Ask** another team member to tap the wave gently with a pencil and **watch** what happens. Now **review** each step in this activity. **Share** and **compare** observations with your research team.

WHAT HAPPENED?

The parts of waves have different names. Look at the illustration in Step 4. See how the paper forms little points — half pointing up, half pointing down? The high spot on each wave is called the **crest**. The low spot is called the **trough**. The distance between two crests or two troughs of a **wave** is called a **wavelength**.

The most important thing about **waves** is their unique ability to carry **energy** from one spot to another. Waves are why we can see, hear, and even feel things that happen some distance away! **Light, sound, electricity** (even television and radio) are the result of energy traveling in waves.

Waves can vary in **amplitude** (height), or in **frequency** (width). Wave characteristics make communication, sight, hearing, and many other things possible.

WHAT WE LEARNED

1 **Describe the Paper Wave pad in Step 1.**
How was it different from the standard sticky pads found in stores?

_____

_____

_____

_____

_____

_____

_____

2 **Describe the Paper Wave pad in Step 2. How was it similar to what it looked like in Step 1? How was it different?**

_____

_____

_____

_____

_____

_____

_____

3 Describe the shadow in Step 3.
What happened when you moved the Paper Wave up and down?

_____

_____

_____

_____

_____

_____

_____

4 What happened when the Paper Wave was tapped on one edge
in Step 4? What was being transferred or carried by the wave?

_____

_____

_____

_____

_____

_____

_____

5 Give three examples of waves carrying energy. Name a kind of wave used
to cook food. (Hint: Most kitchens use this quick heating source.)

_____

_____

_____

_____

_____

_____

_____

CONCLUSION

There are many different kinds of waves — sound waves, light waves, heat waves. Waves can carry various forms of energy. Many wave-related devices play an important role in our lives.

FOOD FOR THOUGHT

John 10:27 Sound waves are an important part of our world. Without sound waves, there would be nothing to hear. It would be difficult to communicate. You would never hear or recognize the voices of your friends or your parents!

Jesus talks about hearing and recognizing his voice. He says that "his sheep" — those who have learned to love and trust him — always know his voice and follow him. If we want to recognize Jesus' words, then we need to spend time with him in study and prayer. Like a special friend, the more time we spend with Jesus, the closer we'll become!

JOURNAL **My Science Notes**

NAME _____

IMAGE BENDER

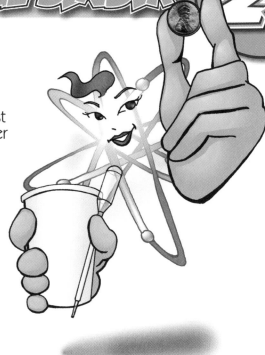

FOCUS Refraction

OBJECTIVE To explore properties of light

OVERVIEW It's a beautiful sunrise. You can just see the tip of the sun peeking over the horizon. Or can you? In this activity, we'll explore how light sometimes deceives us.

WHAT TO DO

STEP 1

Place a coin in a paper cup. **Set** the cup on your work surface and **look** straight down at the coin. Record what you see.

STEP 2

Move the cup to the front edge of your work surface. **Reach** into the cup with one finger and **slide** the coin to the side of the cup opposite you. Now **sit** facing the cup. (Be sure you can still see the coin.) **Record** what you see.

STEP 3

Slowly **lower** your head until you can barely see the coin over the rim of the cup. Now **lower** your head a tiny bit more until the coin disappears. **Freeze** in this position! Now **watch** carefully as a member of your research team gently adds pipettes of water, one at a time.

STEP 4

Look closely at the point where you last saw the coin and **watch** for something to happen. (Note: This activity takes some practice. If nothing happens, repeat Step 3.) **Take turns** participating, then **share** and **compare** observations with your research team.

WHAT HAPPENED?

As you can see from this activity, things aren't always as they appear. The coin looked like it was where it wasn't! The "sun" you see peeking over the horizon at sunrise is really just an **image** of the sun. What causes these illusions? In the case of the sun, its **light** streams strongly toward Earth, but light travels just a bit faster in space than it does in the air. As a result, the light slows down a bit when it hits Earth's **atmosphere**, causing it to "bend."

This bending process is called **refraction**. Just like the water "bent" your view of the coin, the bending of light by the atmosphere makes the sun's image appear slightly higher than the actual sun at sunrise or sunset. (The sun is actually below the horizon.) This refraction also makes the atmosphere act like **lenses** in a telescope, making the sun look a little bigger than normal.

WHAT WE LEARNED

1 Why should you never look directly at the sun? What might happen if you did? Why is it safe to look at the sun's image at sunrise or sunset?

_____

_____

_____

_____

_____

_____

2 Describe Step 2. What does the coin in the cup look like?

_____

_____

_____

_____

_____

3 Describe Step 3. Why do you eventually lose sight of the coin?

4 What happened as the water was added to the cup in step 4? Why?

5 Define refraction. Using the coin or the sun as an example, describe how refraction works.

! CONCLUSION

Light can be bent to form images. The process of light bending is called refraction. This can be demonstrated using water (which also refracts light).

FOOD FOR THOUGHT

Luke 21:8 Were you fooled when the coin's image came up the side of the cup? Sometimes our eyes can really deceive us!

Scripture warns us not to be deceived regarding people who claim they can save us. That goes for things, too! Our world is full of many, many people and things that want to take our time away from God. Even common things like television, sports, or hobbies can fill our minds, leaving no room for God. But don't be deceived by an image of something fun. Only God can fill the longing in your heart and bring you lasting peace and happiness.

JOURNAL My Science Notes

NAME _____

FOCUS Lenses

OBJECTIVE To explore how lenses affect images

OVERVIEW Lenses focus light into images. There are many kinds of lenses (including the ones in your eyes). In this activity, we'll explore how lenses work.

WHAT TO DO

STEP 1

Spread a thin, even coat of petroleum jelly on the flat side of a washer. **Place** the washer in the middle of the microscope slide (jelly side down). Gently **push** down and slightly **twist** the washer to make a watertight seal.

STEP 2

Carefully **place** the microscope slide on the newsprint. **Look** through the center of the washer. **Record** what you see. (Leave the slide in place for the remaining steps.)

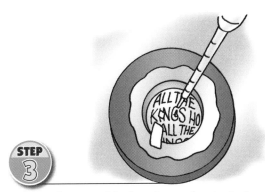

STEP 3

Using a pipette, **add** a few drops of water to the center of the washer. **Continue** adding water until it fills the washer and starts to bulge up like a bubble. Now **look** through the washer again and **record** what you see.

STEP 4

Using the pipette, **pull** water out of the bubble until there is a small dent instead of a bulge. **Look** through the washer again and **record** what you see. **Share** and **compare** observations with your research team.

WHAT HAPPENED?

You made a **lens**, a device that can bend **light**. Actually, you made two different lenses. The bubble (**convex** lens) made the image of the newsprint look larger. The dent (**concave** lens) made the image look smaller.

A lens slows light. The thicker the lens, the slower light travels through it. The slower light travels, the more it bends. Curved shapes help bend light, too. This slowing and bending of light is how lenses work.

If you have glasses or contacts, they also slow and bend light. Notice how the lenses in different glasses often have different shapes. That's because the eye doctor uses different combinations of thickness and shape to slow and bend light just the right amount needed to correct each person's vision problems.

WHAT WE LEARNED

1 **In Step 1, why must the petroleum jelly completely coat the underside of the washer? If it didn't, what might happen when you add water?**

_____

_____

_____

_____

_____

_____

_____

2 **Describe what you observed through the washer in Step 2.**

_____

_____

_____

_____

_____

_____

_____

3 Describe what you observed through the washer in Step 3.
How was this different from Step 2?

_____

_____

_____

_____

_____

_____

4 Describe what you observed through the washer in Step 4.
How was this different from Step 3?

_____

_____

_____

_____

_____

_____

5 What two things does a lens do to light?
Name some things that use lenses to refract light.

_____

_____

_____

_____

_____

_____

CONCLUSION

Lenses slow and bend light to help focus and form images. The shape of a lens (the curvature and thickness) determines what type of image you see.

FOOD FOR THOUGHT

1 Corinthians 13:12 In this activity, you had to set things up very carefully in order for the lens to work properly. Looking through the lens caused the image to change in various ways. You had to get it just right in order to see clearly.

This Scripture reminds us that we see and understand only a little about God now. It's like we're looking through a poorly made lens. Everything we see is kind of hazy and blurred.

Someday we'll see God face to face, and his love will be perfectly clear!

JOURNAL My Science Notes

_____

_____

_____

_____

_____

_____

_____

_____

_____

_____

_____

_____

_____

_____

_____

_____

_____

_____

_____

NAME _____

GOOD VIBRATIONS

LESSON 31

FOCUS Sound

OBJECTIVE To explore how sound is made

OVERVIEW Sound allows us to do many things. It helps us communicate. It helps us avoid danger. It allows us to create music, and to listen to it. In this activity, we'll explore how sound is created.

WHAT TO DO

STEP 1

Remove the paper from the straw and discard. To create a mouthpiece, **slide** the straw's end between your teeth to flatten it, then **snip** off two corners so it looks like the illustration above. **Examine** your "straw flute" and **record** what you see.

STEP 2

To play your straw flute, **buzz** your lips on the mouthpiece like a horn. It takes a little practice. (Your teacher will give you "tune up" time.) Once you've got the hang of it, **blow** a steady tone for about three seconds. **Make notes** about what the tone sounds like.

STEP 3

Carefully **cut** an inch off the end of your flute. Now **repeat** Step 2 with your shortened flute. (Don't forget notes — the written kind!) Now **cut** another inch off your flute and try again. **Notice** the difference. **Predict** what might happen if you shorten your flute even more.

STEP 4

Repeat Step 2 one last time. Now **review** each step in this activity. **Share** and **compare** observations with your research team. Be sure to **discuss** the prediction you made in Step 3 and your reasons for it.

ENERGY · MATTER **137**

WHAT HAPPENED?

Sound is produced by **vibration**. In this activity, you supplied the vibration **energy** by "buzzing." When your lips vibrated, the air inside the tube vibrated, too. The vibrations created **sound waves** your ears heard as the waves moved through the air. Your brain also played a role, remembering the sound and helping you maintain or change it according to your desires.

The length of a vibrating sound wave is the **wavelength**. In this activity, the shorter the tube, the shorter the sound wave or wavelength made. You demonstrated this by changing the length of the straw, which changed the sound.

As the wavelength got shorter, the sound got higher. Musicians call this change in tone **pitch** and scientists call it **frequency** — but the result is the same.

WHAT WE LEARNED

1 **Describe the shape of the straw in Step 1.**
Why does the mouthpiece end have to be shaped so carefully?

_____

_____

_____

_____

_____

_____

2 **Describe the sound your instrument made in step 2.**
Where did the vibration energy come from?

_____

_____

_____

_____

_____

_____

3 How was the sound different in Step 3? What caused this difference?

_____

_____

_____

_____

_____

_____

4 Define "wavelength." In what way do shorter and longer wavelengths sound different?

_____

_____

_____

_____

_____

_____

_____

5 Based on what you've learned, how does the slide on a trombone change sound? What are some other ways musical instruments use vibrations to make sound?

_____

_____

_____

_____

_____

_____

! CONCLUSION

Applied energy can make some objects vibrate. Vibrating objects usually create sound. The pitch (or frequency) of the sound will vary according to the length of the sound wave.

FOOD FOR THOUGHT

Ephesians 5:19 Although the "music" you made in this activity was certainly loud and joyful, it probably wouldn't be very useful for a worship service, would it? But isn't it amazing how many different sounds instruments and voices can make?

Worship is a time we celebrate all that God has done for us. For many people, music makes the worship experience more meaningful. Take time this week to thank those people who make worship music great: the organist, the choir leader, the choir, those who sing or play solos. And don't forget to use your own unique instrument — your voice! Let it speak (or sing) joyful sounds of praise to God.

JOURNAL **My Science Notes**

NAME _____

FOCUS   Static Electricity

OBJECTIVE   To explore static electricity

OVERVIEW   Electricity is something we use every day. But how is electricity made? Is that shock that you get walking across thick carpet a kind of electricity, too? In this activity, we'll explore some properties of static electricity.

WHAT TO DO

STEP 1

Find the "Active Angels" sheet in the back of your work-text (page 173). **Cut out** all the angels and **place** them in a pile. Now carefully **sort** the angels according to size.

STEP 2

Select three angels (different sizes) and **place** them in a petri dish. **Tape** the dish shut. Now **touch** the lid of the dish with the comb. **Record** your observations. (Make sure everyone on your team gets a turn.)

STEP 3

Rub the wool fabric back and forth on the comb rapidly. Now **touch** the lid of the dish with the comb again. **Move** it around slowly. **Record** your observations. (Make sure everyone has a turn.)

STEP 4

Wrap your fingers around the comb. **Slide** it through your palm. **Touch** the lid of the dish again. **Move** the comb around slowly. **Record** what you see. **Share** and **compare** observations with your research team.

?WHAT HAPPENED?

No, the angels weren't "active" by themselves – they needed your help! When you rubbed the comb with the wool, you removed tiny, invisible, **negatively charged electrons** from the **atoms** in the wool. The comb picked these up and held them on its surface, making the entire comb negatively charged. (Your hand provided the **energy** to get the electrons moving. In the process, you made a kind of **electricity** called **static**, or non-moving electricity.)

The "angels" in the container were attracted to the strong negatively charged comb you held near the surface. They overcame the pull of **gravity**, and went flying to the top. Once there, the motion of your comb made them active, moving around on their own. Notice that some angels took their attraction from others, causing the original angels to fall as the new ones took their place!

?WHAT WE LEARNED

1 Why do you think the "angels" in Step 1 had to be very small and lightweight? What would have happened if they were much larger?

_____

_____

_____

_____

_____

_____

2 What did the angels do in Step 2? Why?

_____

_____

_____

_____

_____

_____

3 What did the angels do in Step 3? Why?

_____

_____

_____

_____

_____

_____

_____

4 What did the angels do in Step 4? Why?

_____

_____

_____

_____

_____

_____

_____

5 Sometimes your body can build up static electricity as you walk across a carpet. Based on what you've learned, explain how this happens.

_____

_____

_____

_____

_____

_____

_____

! CONCLUSION

Electricity is a force we use every day. It is based on the movement of electrons. One kind of electricity is static electricity, which builds up as electrons are rubbed off one surface and stick to another.

FOOD FOR THOUGHT

Romans 12:9-11 Static electricity made your angels stick to the lid of the container. It can also makes socks stick together when they come out of the dryer, shock you when you touch a doorknob, or turn a thunderstorm into a heavenly light show! What makes static electricity so "sticky" is the strong attraction between charges.

The strongest attracting force in the universe is God's love! No matter what happens, no matter how dark the night or how scary the situation, God is always holding you tight. Spend time studying his Word, growing to know him better, and you'll find that God's love never lets go!

JOURNAL **My Science Notes**

NAME _____

FOCUS States of matter

OBJECTIVE To explore changes in states of matter

OVERVIEW Everything that surrounds you is made of matter. Ice is a kind of matter that's easily shattered. But in this activity, your teacher will show you a special kind of adhesive that might be used to glue ice back together again.

WHAT TO DO

STEP 1

Set two ice cubes side by side on your work surface. Make sure they are touching each other. **Observe** them for 10 seconds and **record** what you see.

STEP 2

Dip your finger into the "Ice Glue." **Rub** it generously on one side of a cube. Now **rub** it on one side of the other cube. Quickly **place** these two sides together and **lay** the cubes back down. **Observe** them for 10 seconds and **record** what you see.

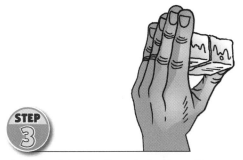

STEP 3

Actually, this "glue" works better with pressure. **Pick up** the ice cubes making sure the "glued" surfaces are touching. **Squeeze** the cubes together tightly and **hold** them together for 20 seconds. (Don't let them move!)

STEP 4

Release the pressure and set the cubes down. **Record** your observations. (If the "glue" didn't work, repeat Step 2.) Now **review** each step in this activity. **Share** and **compare** observations with your research team.

WHAT HAPPENED?

No, there is no such thing as ice glue, although it looked like it for a moment or two! Your ice was a **solid**. To change into a **liquid** state, it needed to absorb some **heat energy**. (Depending on the **temperature** of your classroom, you may have noticed the ice cubes starting to melt a bit in Step 1, but that was just the beginning.)

When you applied **pressure** to the ice cubes, you compressed the ice. This pressure was converted into heat energy, causing the surface of the ice (solid state) to **melt** back into water (liquid state). When you released the pressure, the energy needed to produce the heat was gone. However, the ice cubes were still very cold — cold enough to **refreeze** the thin skin of water between the cubes back into ice. This is what made the ice cubes stick together. No, it wasn't ice glue, just a **change of state**!

WHAT WE LEARNED

1 Describe Step 1. What happened to the ice cubes in this step?

_____

_____

_____

_____

_____

_____

2 Describe Step 2. What happened to the ice cubes in this step?

_____

_____

_____

_____

_____

_____

3 Describe Step 3. What happened to the ice cubes in this step?

_____

_____

_____

_____

_____

_____

4 Describe Step 4. What happened to the ice cubes in this step?

_____

_____

_____

_____

_____

_____

5 List three examples of materials that you've seen change their state. Be sure to describe both the "before" and the "after" phases.

_____

_____

_____

_____

_____

_____

_____

! CONCLUSION

Matter has more than one form. Matter can change from one state to another, but some form of energy must be applied for this to happen.

FOOD FOR THOUGHT

2 Corinthians 1:8-10 Your ice cubes were under a lot of pressure, but that pressure is what created a change of state to make them cling together!

Paul and Timothy went through some terrible trials while telling people about Jesus. They saw how helpless they were to help themselves. That's what made them rely totally on God! God was able to keep them safe, even in terrible times.

Remember that sometimes problems are God's way of helping you learn to depend on him. Let Jesus be the glue that holds you together in good times and in bad!

JOURNAL My Science Notes

COOLING CRYSTALS

FOCUS Endothermic Change

OBJECTIVE To explore endothermic change

OVERVIEW Matter can change form but still be the same material. This kind of change is called a **physical** change. Energy is always involved in a change, and this activity shows a simple way to assess the flow of energy.

WHAT TO DO

STEP 1

Pour one level capful of ammonium nitrate into a test tube. **Fasten** the lid back on the bottle. **Pass** the bottle to each member of your research team. When it is your turn, **wrap** your fingers around the bottle and **feel** the temperature. **Record** your observations.

STEP 2

Now carefully **pass** the test tube to each member of your team. **Wrap** your hands around the tube and **feel** the temperature as you did with the bottle. **Record** your observations.

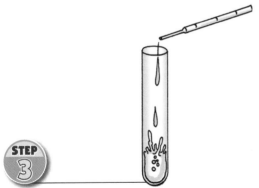

STEP 3

Ask one member of the team to fill a pipette with water. Carefully **pour** the entire pipette of water into the test tube (onto the ammonium nitrate). **Watch** the test tube and **record** your observations.

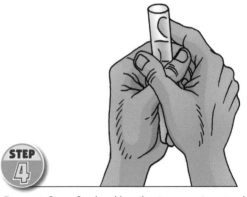

STEP 4

Repeat Step 2, checking the temperature again. **Record** your observations. When everyone has had a turn, clean up as directed by the teacher. Now **review** each step in this activity. **Share** and **compare** observations with your research team.

WHAT HAPPENED?

A **physical change** happens when a material changes its form, but is still the same substance after the change. In this activity, the water **dissolved** the ammonium nitrate creating a **solution** — but the chemical was still the same.

When **matter** changes form, **energy** is always involved. In this case, the water **absorbed** more energy than it **released**. You could tell this by feeling the **temperature** of the test tube — it felt much cooler! This is called an **endothermic** change.

Ammonium nitrate is used in athletes' "ice packs." Many injuries (like a sprain) cause your body to direct fluid to the injured area. This makes it heat up and swell. To decrease swelling, a trainer "cracks" an ice bag, breaking an inner bag that releases water into the chemical. The bag gets very cold, making it draw heat from the injured area.

WHAT WE LEARNED

1 **Describe the bottle's temperature in Step 1.**
What was the chemical in the bottle?

_____

_____

_____

_____

_____

_____

_____

2 **Describe the test tube's temperature in Step 2.**
What was the chemical in the test tube?

_____

_____

_____

_____

_____

_____

3 Describe what happened in Step 3.
Was this a physical or a chemical change? Why?

_____

_____

_____

_____

_____

_____

_____

4 Describe the test tube's temperature in Step 4. Compare Step 2 with
Step 4. What was different about the test tube's contents?

_____

_____

_____

_____

_____

_____

_____

5 Define "physical change." List three examples of materials you've seen
change their physical state. Describe the "before" and "after" phases.

_____

_____

_____

_____

_____

_____

_____

CONCLUSION

Different kinds of changes can occur to matter. These changes always involve energy being taken in or given off. When more energy is absorbed than released (as in this activity), it is called an endothermic change.

FOOD FOR THOUGHT

Matthew 11:28 In this activity, the water absorbed a lot of the excess energy as the matter changed forms. This prevented the test tube from heating up.

Sometimes we're sad and lonely. Our day is filled with problems, and our lives are filled with fears. Our problems seem too much to absorb. But Jesus invites us to let him take our burdens. Instead of heating up with troubles and pain, Jesus can absorb our pain and sorrow, and we can rest in the cooling shadow of his love.

Why not ask Jesus to absorb your burdens right now?

JOURNAL **My Science Notes**

_____

_____

_____

_____

_____

_____

_____

_____

_____

_____

_____

_____

_____

_____

_____

_____

NAME _____

FOCUS Exothermic Change

OBJECTIVE To explore exothermic change

OVERVIEW As we learned in Lesson 34, a physical change occurs when matter changes form but is still the same material. Energy is always involved. This activity continues exploring energy flow.

WHAT TO DO

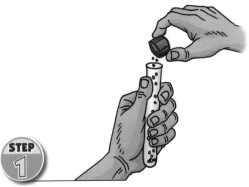

STEP 1

Pour one level capful of calcium chloride into a test tube. **Fasten** the lid back on the bottle. **Pass** the bottle to each member of your research team. When it is your turn, **wrap** your fingers around the bottle and **feel** the temperature. **Record** your observations.

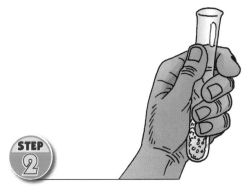

STEP 2

Now carefully **pass** the test tube to each member of your team. **Wrap** your hands around the tube and **feel** the temperature as you did with the bottle. **Record** your observations.

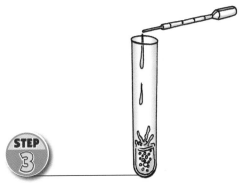

STEP 3

Ask one member of the team to fill a pipette with water. Carefully **pour** the entire pipette of water into the test tube (onto the calcium chloride). **Watch** the test tube and **record** your observations.

STEP 4

Repeat Step 2, checking the temperature again. **Record** your observations. When everyone has had a turn, clean up as directed by the teacher. Now **review** each step in this activity. **Share** and **compare** observations with your research team.

WHAT HAPPENED?

As we learned in Lesson 34, **physical change** happens when a material changes its form, but remains the same substance after the change. Also, whenever **matter** changes form, **energy** is always involved. In this case, the water didn't **absorb** all the energy. You could tell by feeling the **temperature** of the test tube — it felt much warmer! This is called an **exothermic** change.

Although **calcium chloride** is a chemical, and some heat was produced, this was **not** a chemical change. If you were to dry the solution (remove all the water), the material left would still be calcium chloride.

A good example of a **chemical change** that produces heat is **burning**. If you burn a piece of paper, the ashes are completely different from the paper you started with!

WHAT WE LEARNED

1 **Describe the bottle's temperature in Step 1. What was the chemical in the bottle?**

_____

_____

_____

_____

_____

_____

_____

2 **Describe the test tube's temperature in Step 2. What was the chemical in the test tube?**

_____

_____

_____

_____

_____

_____

_____

3 Describe what happened in Step 3.
Was this a physical or a chemical change? Why?

_____

_____

_____

_____

_____

_____

4 Describe the test tube's temperature in Step 4. Compare Step 2
with Step 4. What was different about the test tube's contents?

_____

_____

_____

_____

_____

_____

5 Physical changes involving heat occur all around us.
List three examples. Describe the "before" and "after" phases.

_____

_____

_____

_____

_____

_____

CONCLUSION

Different kinds of changes can occur to matter. These changes always involve energy being taken in or given off. When more energy is released than absorbed (as in this activity) it is called an exothermic change.

FOOD FOR THOUGHT

Romans 12:20-21 It was amazing how hot the test tube got in this activity. Too much heat can be a very painful experience indeed!

So it's pretty surprising that this Scripture says we should heap "coals of fire" on our enemy's head! That sounds pretty mean and extreme, doesn't it?

It goes on to say that the way to do this is to feed him when he's hungry, and give him a drink when he's thirsty. In other words, treat your enemies so well that they are ashamed of how they've been treating you! That's God's way.

JOURNAL My Science Notes

_____

_____

_____

_____

_____

_____

_____

_____

_____

_____

_____

_____

_____

_____

_____

_____

_____

FINDING CHANGE

FOCUS Indicators

OBJECTIVE To explore how an acid or a base affects an indicator

OVERVIEW There are lots of things in nature that change — the colors of leaves, creatures like chameleons, clouds in the sky. As you'll find in this activity, there are even some chemicals that can change!

WHAT TO DO

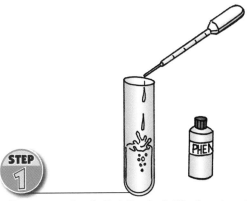

STEP 1

Fill a test tube half full of distilled water. **Open** the phenolphthalein and carefully **add** five drops. **Replace** the lid. Now gently **swirl** the tube to mix the liquid. **Observe** the tube and **record** your observations.

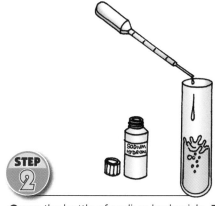

STEP 2

Open the bottle of sodium hydroxide. **Fill** the lid half full. **Draw** sodium hydroxide from the lid with your pipette, then slowly **add** drops to the test tube until the liquid changes color. **Record** your observations.

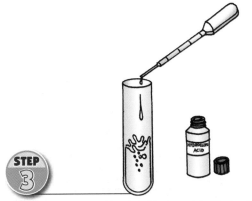

STEP 3

Open the bottle of hydrochloric acid. **Fill** the lid half full. **Draw** hydrochloric acid from the lid with the other pipette (don't use the first one!), then slowly **add** drops to the test tube until there is a change. **Record** your observations.

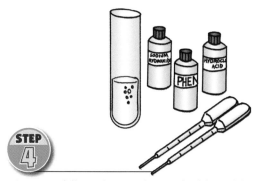

STEP 4

Now carefully **review** each step in this activity, checking the notes you made. **Share** and **compare** observations with your research team.

WHAT HAPPENED?

This experiment shows the effect of an **indicator** on a **solution**. Indicators change their color to show whether something is an **acid** or a **base**. Indicators are chemical "chameleons" with their ability to change color. There are indicators that only change color in an acid, and there are indicators that only change color in a base. Some indicators even change color several times as they go back and forth from acid to base!

Farmers use indicators to test the acid or base content of their fields in order to grow better crops. Doctors and lab personnel use indicators for accurate medical testing. Indicators are even used to check the water quality in your local swimming pool!

With their easily seen color changes, indicators are the perfect tool for many different types of environmental testing and monitoring.

WHAT WE LEARNED

1 Describe the test tube of water in Step 1 before and after the phenolphthalein was added.

_____

_____

_____

_____

_____

_____

_____

2 Describe the test tube of water in Step 2 after the sodium hydroxide was added.

_____

_____

_____

_____

_____

_____

3 Describe the contents of the bottle of hydrochloric acid in Step 3.

_____

_____

_____

_____

_____

_____

4 Describe the test tube of water in Step 4 after
the hydrochloric acid was added.

_____

_____

_____

_____

_____

_____

5 All three chemicals you added were clear. So where did the color
come from in step 3? Why did it go away in step 4?

_____

_____

_____

_____

_____

_____

CONCLUSION

The presence of an acid or a base will cause an indicator to change color. Because their color changes are easy to see, indicators are a great tool for environmental testing and monitoring.

FOOD FOR THOUGHT

Isaiah 1:18 The dark color produced when the sodium hydroxide hit the indicator is just like what sin does to our lives — it stains us! But when the acid was added, the color vanished and the solution was clear.

This is exactly what Jesus does for us! When we accept his death and resurrection, God wipes the stain of sin from our lives. And it doesn't matter what the problem is or how deep and penetrating the darkness of sin — when Jesus comes into our hearts his love covers all, like new fallen snow covering the ground with a fresh, clean blanket of white.

JOURNAL My Science Notes

Poisonous

Non-Poisonous

Copperhead

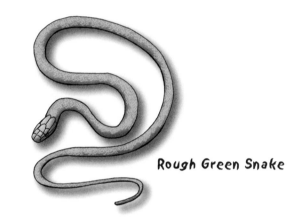

Rough Green Snake

Cottonmouth

King Snake

Rattlesnake

Garter Snake

BUG OUT
LESSON 4

   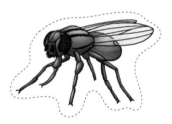

1   1   1   1

1   1   1   1

2   2   2   2

3   3

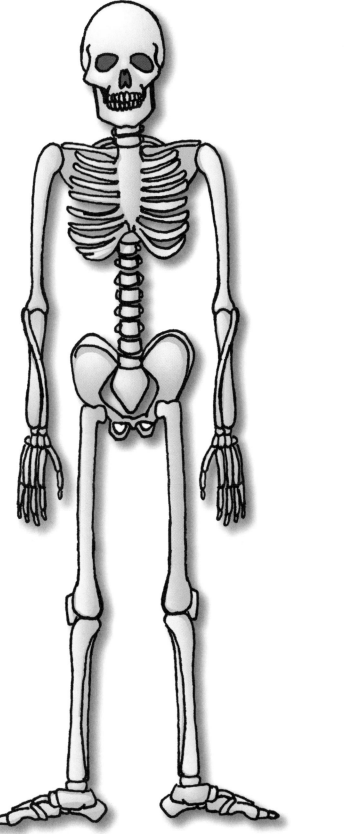

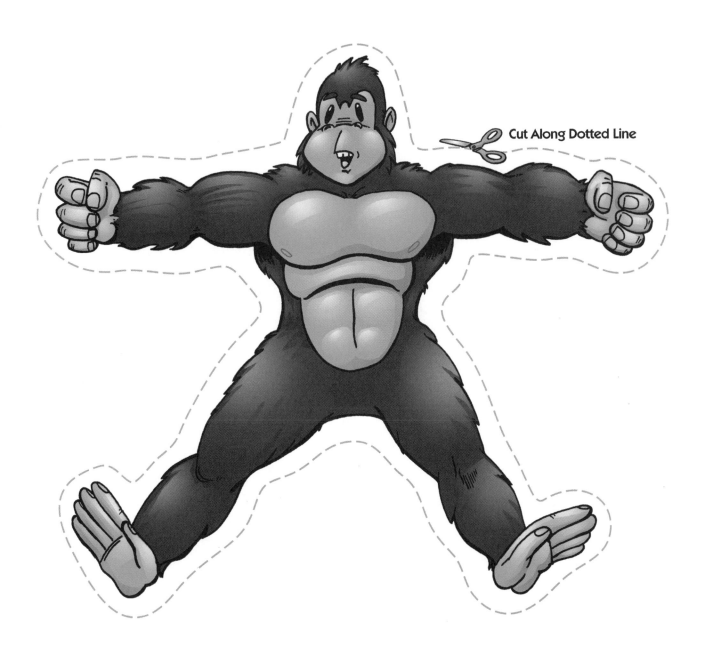

Cut Along Dotted Line

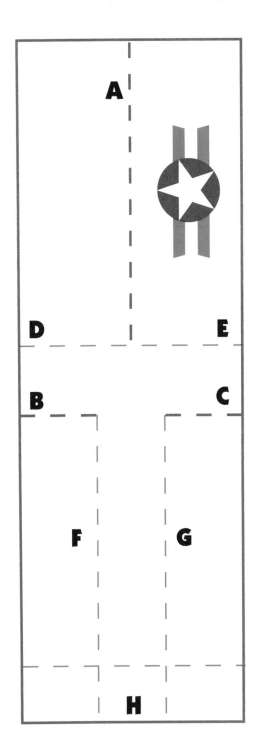

Quick Steps

For detailed steps with illustrations, see page 81.

Step 1

Begin cutting out your **Twisty T** flyer using the solid BLUE lines. (Note: do not cut any RED lines. RED lines are for folding only!)

Step 2

Now cut lines **A**, **B**, and **C** following the dotted BLUE lines. Cut only as far as the lines go! Fold line **D** one way and line **E** the other. (Both emblems should face up!)

Viewed from the side, your **Twisty T** should now look like the letter T.

Step 3

Fold in the sides at lines **F** and **G**. Fold the bottom up at line **H** to make a tab.

Step 4

Launch your **Twisty T** following the instructions on page 81.